CLASSIC SERMONS

ON THE

PRODIGAL SON

KREGEL CLASSIC SERMONS Series

Classic Sermons on Christian Service
Classic Sermons on Faith and Doubt
Classic Sermons on Overcoming Fear
Classic Sermons on Prayer
Classic Sermons on Suffering
Classic Sermons on the Attributes of God
Classic Sermons on the Birth of Christ
Classic Sermons on the Cross of Christ
Classic Sermons on the Prodigal Son
Classic Sermons on the Resurrection of Christ
Classic Sermons on Worship

CLASSIC SERMONS
ON THE
PRODIGAL SON

Compiled by
Warren W. Wiersbe

KREGEL PUBLICATIONS
Grand Rapids, Michigan 49501

Classic Sermons on the Prodigal Son, compiled by Warren W. Wiersbe. © 1990 by Kregel Publications, a division of Kregel, Inc., P. O. Box 2607, Grand Rapids, MI 49501. All rights reserved.

Library of Congress Cataloging-in-Publication Data

Classic Sermons on the Prodigal Son / compiled
by Warren W. Wiersbe.
     p.   cm.— (Kregel classic sermons series)
Includes index.

   1. Prodigal son (Parable)—Sermons. 2. Sermons, English. 3. Sermons, American. I. Wiersbe, Warren W. II. Series: Kregel classic sermons series.

BT378.P8C42   1990   252—dc20   90-30403
                                                  CIP

ISBN   0-8254-4039-4 (pbk.)

2 3 4 5 Printing/Year 95 94 93 92 91

Printed in the United States of America

CONTENTS

PREFACE

THE *KREGEL CLASSIC SERMONS SERIES* is an attempt to assemble and publish meaningful sermons from master preachers about significant themes.

These are *sermons*, not essays or chapters taken from books about themes. Not all of these sermons could be called "great," but all of them are *meaningful*. They apply the truths of the Bible to the needs of the human heart, which is something that all effective preaching must do.

While some are better known than others, all of the preachers, whose sermons I have selected, had important ministries and were highly respected in their day. The fact that a sermon is included in this volume does not mean that either the compiler or the publisher agrees with or endorses everything that the man did, preached, or wrote. The sermon is here because it has a valued contribution to make.

These are sermons about *significant* themes. The pulpit is no place to play with trivia. The preacher has thirty minutes in which to help mend broken hearts, change defeated lives, and save lost souls; and he can never accomplish this demanding ministry by distributing homiletical tid-bits. In these difficult days, we do not need "clever" pulpiteers who discuss the times; we need dedicated ambassadors who will preach the eternities.

The reading of these sermons can enrich your own spiritual life. The studying of them can enrich your own skills as an interpreter and expounder of God's truth. However God uses these sermons in your own life and ministry, my prayer is that His Church around the world will be encouraged and strengthened.

Back to the Bible Broadcast WARREN W. WIERSBE
Lincoln, Nebraska

The Parable of the Prodigal Son

David Martyn Lloyd-Jones (1898-1981) was born in Wales and was taken to London in 1914. There he trained for a medical career and was associated with the famous Dr. Thomas Horder in Harley Street. He abandoned medicine for the gospel ministry, and from 1927 to 1938 he served the Presbyterian Church at Sandfields, Aberavon, Wales. In 1938, he became associate minister with Dr. G. Campbell Morgan at the Westminster Chapel, London; and in 1943, when Morgan retired, Lloyd-Jones succeeded him. His expositions of the Scriptures attracted great crowds wherever he preached. He retired in 1968 to devote his time to writing and limited itinerant ministry. Calvinistic in doctrine, he emphasized the "plight of man and the power of God to save."

This message is reprinted from *Evangelistic Sermons at Aberavon,* published by The Banner of Truth Trust, Carlisle, Pennsylvania and Edinburgh, Scotland and is used by permission of the publishers and the Lloyd-Jones family.

D. Martyn Lloyd-Jones

1

THE PARABLE OF
THE PRODIGAL SON

For this, my son, was dead, and is alive again; he was
lost and is found (Luke 15:24).

THERE IS NO parable or saying of our Lord that is quite
as well-known and as familiar as the parable of the
prodigal son. No parable is quite so frequently quoted
in religious discussions or made use of to support
theories and contentions. It is truly astonishing to note
the almost endless number of ways it is so used and
the almost infinite variety of conclusions to which it is
said to lead. All schools of thought seem to claim a
right to it; that it is used to prove all sorts of theories
and ideas that are mutually destructive and that
exclude one another. It is quite clear, therefore, that
the parable can be very easily and readily mishandled
and misinterpreted. How can we avoid that danger?
What are the principles that should guide us as we
interpret it? It seems to me that there are two
fundamental principles which, if observed, will
guarantee a correct interpretation.

The first is that *we must always beware of interpret-
ing any portion of Scripture in a way that conflicts
with the general teaching of Scripture elsewhere.* The
New Testament must be approached as a whole. It is a
complete and entire revelation given by God through
His servants, a revelation that has been revealed in
parts and sections, all of which go together to make a
complete whole. There are obviously, therefore, no
contradictions among these various parts, no clashes,
no irreconcilable passages and statements. This is not
to say that we can understand every single statement.
What I do say is that there are no contradictions in

Scripture. To suggest that the teachings of Jesus Christ and Paul, or the teachings of Paul and the other apostles, do not agree is subversive of the entire claim of the New Testament itself and of the church's claim for it throughout the centuries, until the rise of the so-called higher-critical school some hundred years ago. I need not go into this matter this evening. Let it suffice to say that it is only the more superficial critics, who are by now many years behind the times, who still try to make and force an antithesis between what they call "the religion of Jesus" and the "faith of St. Paul." Scripture is to be compared with Scripture. Every theory we evolve must be tested by the solid body of doctrine and dogma found in the entire Bible and defined by the church. Were this simple rule remembered, the vast majority of heresies would never have arisen.

The second rule is a little more particular. It is that *we should always avoid the danger of drawing any negative conclusions from the teaching of a parable.* This applies not only to this particular parable, but to all parables. A parable is never meant to be a full outline of truth. Its business is to convey one great lesson, to present one big aspect of positive truth. That being its object and purpose, nothing is so foolish as to draw negative conclusions from it. That certain things are not said in the parable means nothing. A parable is important, and matters only, not from the point of view of what it does not say, but from the point of view of what it does say. Its value is entirely and exclusively positive and in no respect negative.

Now I suggest to you that the failure to remember that simple rule has been responsible for most of the strange and fantastic theories and ideas that have been propounded supposedly on the basis of the parable of the prodigal son. That this should have been possible at all is surely astonishing, for if those who have done this had only looked at the two other parables in the same chapter, they would have seen at once how unjustifiable was their procedure. Why not draw negative conclusions from those also? And so with all parables?

But apart from that, how utterly ridiculous and illogical it is to base your system of doctrine on what is not said. How dishonest it is! It does away with all authority and leaves you with no standard except your own prejudice and your own desire and your own imagination. Now that, I say, is what has been done so frequently with this parable.

Let me illustrate by reminding you of some of the false conclusions that have been drawn from it. Is this not the parable to which they constantly refer who try to prove that ideas of justice and judgment and wrath are utterly and entirely foreign to God's nature and to Jesus' teaching concerning Him? "There is nothing here," they say, "of the father's wrath, nor the father's demands for certain actions on the part of the son—just love, pure love, nothing but love." This is a typical example of a negative conclusion drawn from the parable. Because it does not positively teach the justice and the wrath of God, we are told that such qualities do not belong to God at all. That Jesus Christ elsewhere emphasizes these qualities is of course also completely and entirely ignored.

Another example is the way in which we are told that this parable does away with the absolute necessity for repentance. I have heard of a preacher who tried to prove that the prodigal was a humbug even when he returned home, that he had decided to say something which sounded right, though he did not believe it at all, in order to impress his father, that his exact repetition of the words proves the case. The ultimate point is that in spite of this, in spite of a sham repetition, in spite of all, the father forgave. The final clinching argument of this preacher was that the father said nothing about repentance. Therefore, because he said nothing, repentance does not matter; because repentance is not taught and impressed upon the son by the father, repentance towards God does not matter!

But perhaps the most serious of all the false

conclusions is that which tells us that no mediator between God and man is necessary, and that the idea of atonement is foreign to the gospel and is to be attributed rather to the legalistic mind of Paul. "There is no mention in the parable," they say, "of anyone coming between the father and the son. There is no talk at all about another paying a ransom, or making an atonement; just the direct dealing between father and son conditioned solely upon the latter's return from the far country." Because those things are not specifically mentioned and stressed in the parable, it is agreed that they do not count at all and really do not matter. As if our Lord's object in the parable was to give a complete outline of the whole of the Christian truth, and not just to teach one aspect of the truth. Surely it must be obvious to you that if a like procedure were adopted in the case of all parables, the position would be utterly chaotic. We would be faced with a mass of contradictions.

The business of a parable then is to present to us and to teach us one great positive truth. And if ever that should be clear and self-evident, it is in this particular case. It is no mere accident that this parable is one of three parables. Our Lord seems to have gone out of His way to protect us against the very danger to which I have been referring. But apart even from that, the key to the whole situation is provided in the first two verses of the chapter, which provide us with the essential background and context. "Then drew near unto him all the publicans and sinners to hear him. And the Pharisees and scribes murmured, saying, This man receiveth sinners, and eateth with them" (Luke 15:1–2). Then follow these three parables, obviously dealing with that precise situation and obviously meant to reply to the murmurings of the Pharisees and scribes. And, as if to enforce it still further, our Lord draws a certain moral or conclusion at the end of each parable.

The great point, surely, is that there is hope for all, that God's love extends even to the publicans and sinners. The glorious truth that shines out in these parables, and which is meant to be impressed upon us, is God's amazing love, its scope and its reach. It especially contrasts the ideas of the Pharisees and scribes on that subject.

The first two parables are designed to impress upon us the love of God as an activity which seeks out the sinner, which takes infinite trouble in order to find him and rescue him, and to show the joy of God and all the host of heaven when even one soul is saved. And then comes this parable of the prodigal son. Why this addition? Why the greater elaboration? Why a man, rather than a sheep or a lost coin? Surely there can be but one answer. As the first two parables have stressed God's activity alone without telling us anything about the actions or reactions or condition of the sinner, so this parable is spoken to impress that aspect and that side of the matter, lest anyone should be so foolish as to think that we should all be automatically saved by God's love even as the sheep and the lost coin were found.

The great outstanding point is still the same, but its application is made more direct and more personal. What, then, is the teaching of this parable, what is its message to us this evening? Let us look at it along the following lines.

A Parable of a New Beginning

The first truth it proclaims is *the possibility of a new beginning,* the possibility of a new start, a new opportunity, another chance. The very context and setting of the parable, as I have reminded you already, shows this perfectly. It was because they had sensed and seen this in His teaching that the publicans and sinners drew "near unto Him for to hear Him" (Luke 15:1). They felt that there was a chance even for them, that in this man's teachings there was a new and a fresh hope. And even the Pharisees and scribes saw precisely the same thing. What annoyed them was that our Lord should have had anything at all to do with publicans and sinners. They had regarded such people as being utterly and entirely beyond hope and beyond redemption. That was the orthodox view to take of such people. They were so hopeless that they were to be entirely ignored. Religion was for good people and had nothing at all to do with bad people. It certainly had nothing to give them, and it most certainly did not command good people to mix with bad people and treat them kindly and tell them of new possibilities. So the Pharisees and scribes were annoyed by our Lord's teaching. Anyone who saw any hope for a publican or sinner must, to them, be entirely wrong and a blasphemer. The same point exactly emerges in the parable in the different attitudes of the father and the elder brother toward the prodigal. The point is not how he should be received back, but whether he should be received back, whether he deserved anything at all.

That is what stands out on the very surface. There is a possibility of a new start, a new beginning for all, even for the most desperate. No case can be worse than that of the prodigal son. Yet even he can start again. He has touched bottom, he has sunk to the very dregs, he has gone down so low that he could not possibly descend any further. Never has a more hopeless picture been drawn than that of this boy in the far country amidst the husks and the swine, penniless and friendless, utterly hopeless and forlorn, utterly desolate and dejected. But even he gets a fresh start, even he is called to make a new beginning. There is a turning point that leads on to fortune and to happiness even for him.

What a blessed gospel, and especially in a world like this! What a difference the coming of Jesus Christ has made! What new hope for mankind appeared in Him! There is nothing that so demonstrated and proved that the gospel of Jesus Christ is the only really optimistic philosophy and view of life offered to man, so much as the fact the publicans and sinners drew near to Him to hear Him. And the message they heard, as in this parable of the prodigal son, was something entirely new.

But I would have you note that it was not only new to the Jews and their leaders, but also new to the whole world. The hope held out to the vile and hopeless by the gospel not only cut across the miserable system of the Jews, but also the philosophy of the Greeks. Those mighty men had been evolving their theories and their philosophies. Yet not one of them had anything to offer to the down and out. They all demanded a certain amount of intelligence and moral integrity and purity. They all had to postulate much in the human nature for which they catered. Nor were they realists. They wrote and spoke in a learned and fascinating manner about their utopias and their ideal states, but they left mankind exactly where it was, and were entirely divorced from ordinary life and living. The only people who have ever been in a position even to try the idealistic and humanistic methods of solving the problems of life have been the wealthy and the leisured, and even they have invariably found that they do not work. There was not, and there never had been, any hope for the hopeless in the world before Jesus Christ came. He alone taught the possibility of a new start and a new beginning.

But that teaching was not only new then, during His days on earth, it is still new. And it is still surprising and astonishing and amazes the modern world quite as much as it amazed the ancient world of nearly 2,000 years ago. For the world is still without hope, and its controlling philosophy is still profoundly pessimistic. This is to be seen most clearly, perhaps, when it tries to be optimistic, for we see always that when it tries to comfort us it always has to point us to the future with its unknown possibilities. It tells us that in the new year things surely must be better, that they cannot at any rate be any worse. It argues that the depression must have lasted so long that surely the turn of the tide must of necessity be at hand. It is glad that one year has ended and that a new one is beginning.

What is the real secret of a new year? Its real secret lies in that we know nothing at all about it. All we know is bad, therefore we try to comfort ourselves by looking to what is unknown and by fondly imagining that it must be brighter and better. Then listen to it as it talks about its schemes and plans for the uplift of mankind. All it can tell you is that it is trying to make a better world for its children, trying to build for the future and for posterity. Always in the future! It can do nothing for itself, it can only hope to make things better for those who are yet unborn. And the longer it goes on talking about that and trying to do it, the more hesitant does it become. To prove this, just compare the language of 1875 with that of 1935, or even that of 1905 with 1935.

But if the situation is like that with regard to society in general and at large, how infinitely more hopeless and filled with despair is it when we face it in a more individual and in a more personal sense! What has the world to offer by way of solution to the problems that tend to distress us most of all! The answer to that question is to be seen in the frantic efforts that men and women are making in their attempts to solve their problems. And yet nothing is more clearly seen than the fact that all their attempts are failures.

Year after year men and women make their new resolutions. They realize that above all else what is needed is a fresh start and a new beginning. They decide to turn their backs on the past, to turn over a new leaf, or even to start a new book of life. That is their desire, that is their firm conviction and intention. They want to break with the past and for a time they do their utmost to do so, but it doesn't last. Gradually but inevitably they slide back to the old position and to the old state of affairs. And after a few such experiences they no longer try, and come to the conclusion that all is hopeless. Up to a point, the fight is kept up and maintained, but sheer weariness and fatigue eventually overcome them, the pressure and the might of the world and its way seem to be entirely on the other side and they give in. The position seems to be utterly hopeless.

I wonder how many there are, even in this service

now, who feel like that in some respect or other! Do you feel that your life had gone wrong, has gone astray? Are you forever mocked by "the haunting spectre of the might-have-been?" Do you feel that you have got yourself into such a position, and into such a situation, that you can never get out of it and put yourself right again? Do you feel that you are so far away from what you ought to be, and from what you would like to be, that you can never get there again? Do you feel hopeless about yourself because of some situation with which you are confronted, or because of some entanglement in which you have got involved, or because of some sin which has mastered you and which you cannot conquer? Have you turned to yourself and said, "What is the use of making any further effort, what is the use of trying again? I have tried and tried many and many a time before, but all to no purpose, and my trying now can lead to but the same result. I have made a mess of my life, I have forfeited my chance and my opportunity, and henceforth I have nothing to do but to make the best of a bad job."

Are such your thoughts and your feelings? Is it your position that you have missed your opportunity in life, that what has been has been, that if only you have another chance things might be different, but that cannot be, and there it is? Is it that? Alas! How many there are in such a position. How unhappy are the lives of the average man and woman. How hopeless! How sad!

Now the very first word of the gospel to people like that is that they should lift up their heads, that all is not lost, that there is still hope, still the possibility of a new start and a new beginning, here and now without any delay at all, and without looking to the slightest extent on something imaginary that may belong to the unknown future, but rather by leaning on something that happened in the past nearly 2,000 years ago, but which is as strong and as powerful today as it was then. Even the prodigal can get right. There is a possible turning point even along the blackest and the most hopeless road. There is a new beginning offered even to the publicans and sinners.

Conditions Attached

But I must hasten to point out in detail what I have already indicated in passing, that this message of the gospel is not something vague and general like the world's message, *but something to which definite conditions are attached.* And it is here we see most clearly why it was that our Lord spoke this particular parable in addition to the other two. To avail ourselves of this new beginning and new start which is offered by the gospel, we must observe the following points. Oh! let me impress upon you the importance of doing this. If you merely sit there and listen and allow yourselves to be moved in general by the glowing picture of the gospel, you will go home exactly as you were when you came. But if, on the other hand, you attend carefully and note each point and act upon it, you will find yourself going home an entirely different person. If you are anxious to avail yourself of the gospel's new hope and new start, you must follow its methods and instructions. What are they?

The first is that we must face our position squarely, honestly and truly. It is one thing to be in a bad and difficult position, it is quite a different thing to face it honestly. This prodigal son had been in a thoroughly bad situation for a very long time before he truly realized it. A man does not suddenly get into that state in which he is described here. It happened gradually, almost unbeknown to himself. And even after it happened, he did not properly realize it for some time. The process is so quiet and so insidious that the man himself scarcely sees it at all. He looks at his face in the mirror every day and does not see the changes that are taking place. It is someone who only sees him at intervals who sees the effects most clearly. And often when we begin to sense our terrible plight, we deliberately avoid thinking about it. We brush such thoughts aside and busy ourselves with other matters, more or less saying to ourselves as we do so, "What's the use of thinking, here I am anyhow." But the very first step back is to face the issue, to face the situation honestly and clearly. We are told that this young man "came to himself" (v. 17). That is actually what the man did! He faced things out with himself and did so quite frankly. He saw that his troubles were entirely due to his own actions, that he had been a fool, and that he should never have left his father, and should certainly never have treated him as he had done. He looked at himself and could scarcely believe that it really was himself. He looked at the husks and at the swine. He faced it directly.

Have you done that? Have you really looked at yourself? What if you put all your actions of the past year down on paper? What if you had kept a record of all your thoughts and desires, your ambitions and imaginings? Would you consent to their publication with your name beneath them? What are you now in comparison with what you once were? Look at your hands, are they clean? Look at your lips, are they pure? Look at your feet, where have they trodden, where have they been? Look at yourself! Is it really you? Then look around you at your position and surroundings! Do not shirk it! Be honest! What are you living on? Is it food or swine's husks?

On what have you spent your money? For what purpose have you used money that should perhaps have gone to feed your wife and children or to clothe them? On what have you been living? Look! Is it food fit for men? Look at what you enjoy. Face it calmly. Is it worthy of a creature created by God with intelligence and understanding? Does it honor man, let alone God? Is it swine's food or is it really fit for human consumption? It is not enough that you should just bemoan your fate or feel miserable. How did you ever get into such a state and condition? Look at the swine and the husks and realize that it is all because you have left your Father's house, that you have deliberately gone against your conscience, deliberately flouted religion and all its commands and dictates, that it has been entirely and utterly of your own doing. You are where you are today entirely as the result of your own choice and your own actions. Face that and admit it. That is the first essential step on the way back.

The next is to realize that there is only One to whom you can turn and only one thing to do. I need not work out that point in detail in connection with the prodigal. It is perfectly clear. "No man gave unto him" (v. 16). He had tried and had exhausted his own efforts and the efforts of all other people.

He was finished and no one could help him. There was but one left. Father! The last, the only hope. The gospel always insists upon our coming to that point. As long as you have a penny of your own left, the gospel will not help you. As long as you have friends or agencies to which you can apply for help and which you believe can help you, the gospel will give you nothing. Actually, of course, as long as a man thinks he can keep himself going by some of these other methods, he will continue to try to do so. And the world is far from being bankrupt in our estimation still. It still believes in its own methods and ideas.

How pathetically we cling to them! We bank on our own willpower and our own efforts. We draw upon the new years of our calendar as if they made the slightest difference to the actual state of affairs! We invoke the aid of friends and companions and of relations and dear ones. Ah! you know all about the process, not only in your attempts to put yourself right, but also in your attempts to put others right about whom you are concerned and worried. And on we will go until we have exhausted all. Like the prodigal, we go on until we become frantic and until "no man give unto us." Then and then only do we turn to God. Oh! how foolish.

Let me try to explode the fallacy here and now. Face it frankly. Realize that all your efforts must fail as they have always failed. Realize that the improvement will only be transient and temporary. Cease to fool yourself. Realize how desperate the position is. Realize further that there is only one power that can put you right—the power of Almighty God. You can go on trusting yourself and others and trying with all our might. But a year from tonight the position will not only be the same, but actually worse. God alone can save you.

But as you turn to Him, you must realize further *that you can plead nothing before Him except His mercy and His compassion.* As the prodigal left home, his great word was "give."

He demanded his rights. He was full of self-confidence, and he even had a feeling that he was not being given his due and his rights. "Give!" But when he returns home, his vocabulary has changed and his word now is "make." Before, he felt he was someone and somebody and something which could demand rights worthy of itself and of himself. Now he feels he is nobody and nothing and realizes that his first need is to be made into something. "Make me!" he said.

If you feel that you have any right to demand pardon and forgiveness from God, I can assure you that you are damned and lost. If you feel that it is God's business and God's duty to forgive you, you will most certainly not be forgiven. If you feel God is hard and against you, you are guilty of the greatest sin of all. If you feel still that you are somebody and that you have a right to say "give," you will receive nothing but misery and continued wretchedness.

But if you realize that you have sinned against God and angered Him; if you feel you are a worm and less, and unworthy even of the name of man, quite apart from being unworthy of God; if you feel you are just nothing in view of the way you have left Him and turned your back upon Him, and ignored Him and flouted Him; if you just cast yourself upon Him and His mercy, asking Him if in His infinite goodness and kindness He can possibly make something of you, all will be different. God never desired to see you as you now are. It was against His wish and His will that you have wandered away. It is all of your own doing. Tell Him so and tell Him further that what worries and distresses you most of all is not merely the misery you have brought upon yourself, but the fact that you have disobeyed Him and insulted Him and wronged Him.

Then having realized all this, *act upon it*. Leave the far country. You have stood up in the field of the swine and the husks by your mere action in visiting this chapel. But walk right out of that far country. Leave the swine and the husks. Turn your back on sin and give yourself to God. Feelings and desires and inclinations will avail you nothing.

Do it!

Make a break.

Get to God and get right with God!

Take your stand.

Commit yourself!

Venture on Him!

Trust Him!

How ridiculous it would have been for the prodigal to have thought of all he did and yet not do it! He would still have remained in the far country. But he did it. He acted upon his decision. He carried out his resolution. He went to his father and cast himself upon his mercy and compassion. You must do the same in the way I have already indicated.

An Amazing Discovery

If you but do so, you will find that in your case, as in the case of the prodigal, *there will be a real, solid new beginning and new start*. The impossible will happen and you will be amazed and astounded at what you will discover. I pass over the joy and the happiness and the thrill of it all tonight, in order that I may impress upon you the reality of the new start which the gospel gives. It is not something light and airy. It is no mere matter of sentiment or feelings. It is no mere drug or anesthetic which dulls our senses and therefore makes us dream of some bright realm. It is real and actual. In Jesus Christ a real genuine new start and new beginning are possible. And they are possible alone in Him!

The greatness of the father's love in the parable is seen not so much in his attitude as in what he did. Love is no mere vague sentiment or general disposition. Love is active. It is the mightiest activity in the world and it transforms everything. That is why here also, the love of God alone really can give us a new start and a new chance. The love of God does not merely talk about a new beginning, it makes a new beginning. "God so loved the world that He *gave*" (John 3:16). The father did things to the prodigal; God alone can do that to us and for us which can set us on our feet again. Let us observe how He does it. Oh! the wondrous love of God that really makes all things new and that alone can do so.

Observe how the father blots out the past. He goes to meet the son as if nothing had ever happened. He embraces him and kisses him as if he has always been most dutiful and exemplary in all his conduct! And how quickly he commands the servants to strip off the rags and the tatters of the far country and remove from his son every trace and vestige of his evil past. He wipes out the past by all those actions, in a way that no one else could do. He alone could forgive really, he alone could wipe out what the boy had done against the family and against himself, and he did so. He strips off every trace of the past.

That is always the first thing that happens when a sinner turns to God in the way we have been describing. We go to Him and expect just as little as the prodigal who had expected to be made a servant. How infinitely does God transcend our highest expectations when He begins to deal with us. All we ask for is a kind of new beginning. God amazes and surprises us, in His very first action, by blotting out our past. And that, after all, is what we desire most of all. How can we be happy and be free in view of our past? Even if we no longer do a certain action, or commit a particular sin, there is a past, there is what we have done already. That is the problem.

Who can deliver us from our past? Who can erase from the book of our life what we have done already? There is but One! And He can! The world tries to persuade me that it does not matter, that I can turn my back upon it and forget it. But I cannot forget it; it keeps on returning. And it makes me miserable and wretched. I try everything, but still my past remains, a solid, awful, terrible fact. Can I never get free from it? Can I ever be rid of it?

There is only One who can strip it off my back. I only know that my rags and tatters have really gone when I see them on the Person of Jesus Christ the Son of God who wore them in my stead and became a curse in my place. The Father commanded Him to take my filthy rags off me, and He has done so. He bore my iniquity, He clothed and covered Himself with my sin. He has taken it away and has drowned it in the sea of God's forgetfulness. And when I see and believe that God in Christ has not only forgiven but also forgotten my past, who am I to try to look for it and to find it? My only consolation when I consider the past is that God has blotted it out. No one else could do so. But He has done so. It is the first essential step in a new beginning. The past must be erased, and in Christ and His atoning death, it is!

But in order to have a really new start, I require something further. It is not enough that every trace of my past be removed. I require something in the present. I desire to be clothed, I must be robed. I need confidence to start afresh and to face life and its people and its problems. Though the father met the boy and kissed him, that alone would not have given him confidence. He would have known that everyone was looking at the rags and at the mud. But the father does not stop at that. He clothes the boy with a dress that is worthy of a son, and he places a ring on his finger. He gives him the status of a son and the external proofs of that station. He announces to all that his son has returned, and so clothes him as to make him feel unashamed when he meets people. No one else could do that but the father. Others could have taken the boy in and have helped him, but no one could make him a son but the father. No one else could give him his position and provide him with the wherewithal.

It is precisely the same with us when we turn to God. He not only forgives and blots out the past, He makes us sons. He gives us new life and new power. He will so assure you of His love that you will be able to face others unashamed. He will clothe you with the robe of Christ's righteousness, He will not only tell you that He regards you as a child, but make you feel that you are one. As you look at yourself, you will not know yourself. You will look at your body and see this priceless robe; you will look at your feet and see them newly shod; you will look at your hand and see the ring and signet of God's love. And as you do so, you will feel that you can face the whole world without apology, yes, and face the devil also, and all the powers that fooled you in the past and ruined your life. Without this standing and confidence, a new start is a mere figment of the imagination. The world only tries to clean the old suit and make it look respectable. God in Christ alone can clothe us with the new robe and really make us strong. Let the world try to point its finger and remind us of our past. Let it do its worse; we have but to look at the robe and the shoes and the ring, and all is well.

And if you require a clear proof of the actuality of all this, it is to be found in the fact that even the world has to acknowledge that it is true. Listen to the servant speaking to the elder brother. What does he say? Is it, "A strange-looking man in rags and tatters has come from somewhere?" No! "Thy brother is come" (15:27). How did he know he was the brother? Ah! he had seen the father's actions and had heard the father's words. He would never have recognized the son, but the father did, even while he was yet a long way off. The father knew!

And God knows you. When you go to Him and allow Him to clothe you, everyone will get to know it. Even the elder brother knew it. It was the last thing he wanted to know, but the conclusion to be drawn from the singing and the noise of jubilation and happiness was unavoidable. He is too mean to say "my brother," but he, even he, has to say "this thy son." I do not promise that everyone will like you and speak well of you if you give yourself to God in Christ. Many will certainly hate you and persecute you and try to laugh at you and do many things to you, but, in doing so, they will actually be testifying that they also have seen that you are a new man and that you have been made anew and have been given a new start.

Come!

Here is an opportunity for a real new beginning. It is the only way. God Himself has made it possible by sending His only begotten Son into this world, to live and die and rise again. It matters not at all what you have been, nor what you are like at the moment. You have but to come to God confessing your sin against Him, casting yourself upon His mercy in Jesus Christ, acknowledging that He alone can save and keep, and you will find that

The past shall be forgotten,
A present joy be given,
A future grace be promised,
A glorious crown in heaven.

Come! Amen.

NOTES

The Prodigal Son

Dwight Lyman Moody (1837-1899) is known around the world as one of America's most effective evangelists. Converted as a teenager through the witness of his Sunday school teacher, Moody became active in YMCA and Sunday school work in Chicago while pursuing a successful business career. He then devoted his life to evangelism and was used mightily of God in campaigns in both the United States and Great Britain. He founded the Northfield School for Girls, the Mount Hermon School for Boys, the Northfield Bible Conference, and the Moody Bible Institute in Chicago. Before the days of planes and radio, Moody traveled more than a million miles and addressed more than 100 million people.

This message is from *The Gospel Awakening*, edited by L.T. Remlap, and published in 1879 in Chicago by J. Fairbanks and Company.

Dwight L. Moody

2

THE PRODIGAL SON

I will arise and go to my father, and will say unto him,
Father, I have sinned against heaven, and before thee
(Luke 15:18).

WE HAVE FOR our subject tonight "The Prodigal Son."
Perhaps there is not any portion of Scripture that this
audience is so familiar with as this fifteenth chapter of
Luke. These boys down here in the audience can tell
the story as well as I can. All the Sunday school children
know this chapter as well as I do. In the second verse
we are told why Christ described this beautiful picture.
The Pharisees and scribes were murmuring, and they
said, "This man receiveth sinners, and eateth with
them." They told the truth for once. An angel from
heaven could not have told the truth plainer then they
did when they said, "This man receiveth sinners, and
eateth with them." That is what Christ came into the
world for. And while they were complaining, He went
on and gave us three parables: the lost sheep, the lost
piece of money, and the lost son.

The Prodigal's Trouble

This young man, the prodigal son, started wrong—
that was the trouble with him. He was like hundreds
and thousands of young men in our cities today, who
have a false idea of life. When a man has a false idea
of life, it is very hard for his father or mother or any
friends to do anything with him. I do not know where
his mother was. Perhaps he had sent her to the grave
with a broken heart. The Lord did not speak of his
mother; if she had been living, he would have referred
to her. The father is to be censured; we cannot help
but blame the father. When the son said, "Father, give

me my portion" (v. 12), the father should have said,
"You show a bad spirit. I will let you go without your
portion." A great many fathers make that mistake now.
I do not think the father could have done a greater
unkindness to the boy than to give him his goods and
money, and let him go. It showed a contemptible spirit
in the boy when he came to his father and said, "Divide:
give me my portion and let me go." He wanted to go
away from his father's prayers and influence. He wanted
to get into a foreign land where he could go on as he
pleased, where he could run riot and plunge into all
kinds of sin, and where there was no restraint. And
that indulgent father gratified his wish and divided
his goods with him. Not many days later, he went
around to his old companions and bade them all
goodbye, and went off to a foreign country, perhaps to
Egypt. While he was there, his family must have heard
from him, because the eldest brother said, "This brother
hath spent all with harlots, and thou hast killed for
him the fatted calf" (v. 30).

Undoubtedly, the first time they heard from him
they heard bad news. I can see him going away very
proud: you might as well talk to an iron post as to talk
to him now. He is full of conceit and false ideas. He is
going to get on without his father or any help from his
friends; he will have no trouble, in his own mind. But
the very first thing we hear of him is, he is in bad
company. I never knew a young man who treated his
father unkindly but would go right off into bad company.
He got into the far country, and now we hear of him
going on in all kinds of vice.

Undoubtedly, if they had theaters in those days, and
I do not doubt but they had, he would be in the theater
every night in the week. We would find him in the
billiard hall and the drinking saloon. We do find him
in the ways of those whose feet take hold on hell. He
was a popular young man; he had plenty of money,
and his money was popular. He was a grand companion
for the young men in that far country; they liked his
society. I do not know how long he had been there; but

I do not suppose it was more than 5 years, and perhaps not more than 3 years. It does not take long for a young man to go to ruin when he gets in among thieves and harlots: that is about the quickest way down to hell. At last his money is gone, and now his friends begin to drop off, one after another. He is not quite so popular as he was when he had plenty of money. He is getting a little shabby; his clothes are not so good as they were. He had a good wardrobe; but now he goes to the pawnshop, and he pawns his overcoat. I have seen a good many such young men in Philadelphia. I think his overcoat is gone for strong drink; and one thing after another soon goes. He might have had some gift that his mother gave him when she was dying, and at last that goes; and yet he does not come to himself.

The very first thing he did do that I like to commend was that he joined himself to a citizen of that country to find some work to do. That is the noblest thing he did. There is some hope for a man when he is willing to go to work. I have more hope for the gambler, the harlot, the drunkard, and for any class of people, than I have for a lazy man. I never knew a lazy man to be converted yet. The prodigal started to get some work to do, even if it was to feed swine. That is the lowest occupation a Jew could be engaged in. He joined himself to a citizen of the country and fed swine; and he would have eaten the husks if he could have got them. No man gave him even husks. This wealthy man's son, who was brought up amid good influences and surroundings, is now living in that foreign country like a man who had never seen a decent home.

What the Prodigal Lost

Now, just for a moment think what that man lost in all these years. *He lost his home;* he has no home. His friends, when he had money, might have invited him around to their homes; but it is no home for him. There was no loving home. There is not a prodigal upon the face of the earth but has lost his home. You may live in a gilded palace; but if God is not there, it is no home. If your conscience is lashing you, it is no home.

He lost his food; his father's table did not go to that country. He would have fed on the husks that the swine did eat; but no one gave unto him. This world cannot satisfy the soul.

Then *he lost his testimony.* I can imagine some of the young men of that country saw him among the swine, feeding them and taking the place of a shepherd's dog among them; and they said, "Look at that poor wretched young man, with no shoes on his feet, and with such shabby garments." They looked at him and called him a beggar, and pointed the finger of scorn at him. He said, "You need not call me a beggar; my father is a wealthy man." They said, "Your father a wealthy man?" "Yes." "You look like a wealthy man's son!" There was not a man who believed him when he said he was a wealthy man's son. His testimony was gone; no one would believe him. So when a man goes in the service of the devil, he sinks lower and lower; and it is not long before everyone loses confidence in him. One sin leads on to another. His testimony is gone.

But there is one thing he did not lose, and if there is a poor backslider here tonight, there is one thing you have not lost. *That young man never lost his father's love.* I can imagine one of his father's neighbors has met him in that place, and says to him, "My boy, I have just come from your home; your father wants you to go home." I can imagine the young man said, "Did my father speak of me? I thought he had forgotten me." "Why," says the man, "he doesn't think of anything else; he thinks of you day and night. Do you think he has forgotten you? No, never. He cannot forget you; he loves you too well for that." He didn't yet come to himself; there he is.

Thinking of Home

But one day, I can see him, he gets a-thinking. It is a good thing to stop and think. I wish we could get some of the men in Philadelphia to think where they are, and what is going to be the end of it. He begins to think that over those blue hills there is a home; and there is a father in that home, who loves him still. As the Scripture puts it, "He came to himself" (v. 17). It is a grand thing to see a man coming to himself. When he began to come to himself, then there was hope for him. It teaches us clearly that all these years he has been out of his mind. Very likely he thought Christians were out of their minds. There is not a drunkard, harlot, thief, or gambler, but thinks Christians are mad; and they call us fanatics. But Solomon says, "Madness is in their heart while they live, and after that they go to the dead" (Eccl. 9:3).

The prodigal, perhaps, sends word: "I have spent all my money, I wish you would send me some money." The father says, "I will not give him any more money; for, if I do, he will go on with his riotous living." Some men think God does not love them because He does not answer their prayers while they are living in sin. The father loved the boy too well to send him any money.

There was a mother who came to me not long ago with a prodigal boy. She wanted me to talk and pray with him. I said, "You have come to the wrong person; why don't you take him to Christ?" She said she had. I found this boy was the son of a wealthy father; and he had been brought up to do nothing, and he had all the money he wanted. I said, "This boy has the false idea that all he has got to do is, to write to his father for money." I said, "You make a great mistake. Do you think the prodigal son would have come home if his father had given him all the money he wanted? He never would have come home if he had not gotten to the end of his rope."

When the prodigal came to himself, he said, "I will perish here. I will arise and go to my father" (vv. 17, 18). And that was the turning point in this young man's life. There is always hope for a man when he begins to think. I wish you would bear in mind that, if you are willing to own your sin, and confess that you have wandered from God, God is willing to receive you. The very moment you are willing to come, that moment God is willing and ready to receive you. He delights in forgiveness. I do not care how vile you have been, if you are willing to come back, God is willing and ready to receive you.

The turning point was when he came to himself, and said, "How many hired servants of my father's have bread enough and to spare, and I perish with hunger. I will arise and go to my father, and say unto him, 'Father, I have sinned against heaven and before thee.'" I can imagine the angels hovering over him as he said this; and an angel wings his way to heaven and says, "Ring the bells of heaven!" "There is joy in heaven over one sinner that repenteth." He rises like a man; his mind is made up. He has his heart set upon one thing, "I am going home." It did not take long, after he had made up his mind, to go; he had not many friends to go and bid goodbye. They had gotten all he had in that country, and now there was no one there to love and pity him; there was no one there to care for him. But he knew there was one solitary man that would love him, if anyone would on earth; and that man was his father.

There is a God in heaven who will love you and pity you, and have mercy on you, if you will come to Him. There may be a hiss go up. The Pharisees may look down with contempt upon you; they may pass you on the street and not speak to you; but there is a God who takes care of you, and who is willing to blot out your sin, if you are willing to come to him. The blessed Master brought out this parable to teach the lesson of the Father's love.

A Never-dying Love

There was a young man who went off to California, and he left behind a kind, praying father. He went to the Pacific coast; and the first letter to his father brought the tidings that he was in bad company. The next letter told that he had gone on from bad to worse; and every time the father heard from that boy he heard how he was going on in sin. At last one of the neighbors was going out to California, and the father said to him, "When you get there hunt up my boy, and tell him one thing—that his father loves him still. Tell him my love is unchanged. Tell him I never loved him more than I do at the present time; and if he will come home, I will forgive him all."

When the man got to California, he had hard work to find the boy. But one night, past midnight, he found him in one of the lowest dens in California. He got him out, and he said to him, "I have news from home for you. I have come from New England, and just before I left I met with your father. He told me, if I found you, to tell you that he loved you as much as ever, and he wants you to come home." The young prodigal said, "Did my father tell you to tell me he loved me still? I do not understand that." "But," says the man, "it is true." That broke the man's heart, and he started back to his father.

I bring the message to you that God loves you still. I say to every sinner in Philadelphia, I do not care how vile you are in the sight of your fellowmen, I want to tell you upon the authority of God's Word, that the Lord Jesus loves you, and loves you still.

I see the prodigal son: He starts for home, and he has a hard journey of it; he is almost starved. There has been a famine in that land; perhaps the famine struck that land to bring that man back to his father's house. Many a trouble comes upon us to bring us to God. He is coming along over the highway, and night comes on; he sleeps. Day after day he travels on. He has no fears of thieves troubling him, for he had squandered all in that foreign land.

As he crosses the line that brings him into his native country, his heart must have beat quicker and quicker. This thought might have come to him: "Perhaps my father is dead, and then no one will love me. It may be my father will not receive and forgive me." He might have thought that, as his father had refused to give him money, he would not receive him. Still he comes on. I see him coming in sight of that old homestead. Perhaps some of you understand his feelings. Perhaps some of you have been away for years, and then, when you came back to the old homestead, the tears would come trickling down your cheeks as you remembered the first morning when you left home.

When a young man leaves home, the thought will come across him that he may never return. This boy has been away for years. He is coming home; he sees the playground. He is sick of that foreign country; he is sick of that devil's own country; it has not satisfied him. I never yet have seen a man who lived for the world and was satisfied. He has this thought: "I wonder if my father will let me come in. I will ask him to let me get in among the servants."

I can see the old man; he is up there on the flag-roof of the house. It is in the cool of the day; the sun is sinking down behind those Palestine hills. He is looking in the direction his boy went away years ago. How his heart has ached for him; how he has loved him. I can see the old man as he looks, and as he sees that boy coming back. He cannot recognize him by his dress; but love is keen to detect its object, and he can see it is his darling boy.

He comes down those stairs, and he sweeps out past the servants, as if the spirit of youth had come back upon him. You can see his gray hairs, as he flies through the air and leaps over the highway. He runs and leaps for joy. The boy begins to speak, but the father will not hear him. He takes the boy's hand and says, "Bring out the best robe and put it on him. Put a ring on his hand. Bring out shoes and put on his feet, and kill the fatted calf; and let us eat and be merry" (vv. 22, 23).

I see the old man weeping tears of joy. In that home there is gladness. The boy is eating that sumptuous meal; he has not had as good a meal for many a year. It seems almost too good to be true. Picture the scene. While he is there he begins to weep; and the old man, who is weeping for joy, looks over to him and says, "What are you weeping for." The boy says, "Well, father,

I was thinking it would be an awful thing if I should leave you again, and go into a foreign country." But if you sit down at God's feast, you will not want to go back into the devil's country again.

Oh, my friends, tonight come home. God wants you; his heart is aching for you. I do not care what your past life has been. This night, upon the authority of God's Word, I proclaim salvation to every sinner. They said of Jesus, "This man receiveth sinners, and eateth with them." Every sinner has a false idea of God; he thinks God is not ready and willing to forgive him. He says it is not justice. But God wants to deal in mercy. If the old man had dealt in justice, he would have barred the door and said to his son, "You cannot come in my house." That is not what fathers are doing. Their doors are not barred against their own children. Their doors are wide open, and they bid you come home. There is no father in Philadelphia who has as much love in his heart as God has for you. You may be black as hell; yet God stands ready and willing to receive you to His bosom, and to forgive you freely.

No One Too Far Gone

Two weeks ago last Sunday, there was a poor, fallen woman who came to this meeting; and I would to God we had more come in. I would like to see every fallen woman come to Jesus. I would like to preach to the 2,000 fallen woman in this city; I would like to tell them how Jesus would forgive them. The sermon did not touch this woman until I got to that part where I said, There was no sinner so vile but Jesus would receive that one; and it went like an arrow to her soul. She came to the inquiry-room, and made up her mind never to go back. In the course of 48 hours, she found her way to the feet of Jesus, and her heart went out with others.

She thought of another; and thanks be to God, she is here tonight. There were two Christian ladies who left this city this morning to see the mother; and when they came to her house, she was not going to let them in. She was sick, and did not want to receive any callers; but the thought came to her that perhaps they were bringing good news from her husband. When these two angels of light came in, they said they came to talk about her daughter Mary. The woman said, "My daughter; have you brought news of my child? Where is she? Oh, how my heart has ached for 15 long years. Why did you not bring her with you?" They said, "We did not know if you would receive her." She said, "Oh, how my heart has been aching. Won't you bring her back tomorrow morning?" If the mother will receive that child, do you tell me God will not receive her? There is not a poor sinner here tonight God will not receive.

William Dawson, the celebrated Yorkshire farmer, once said that there was no man so far gone in London that Christ would not receive him. A young lady called on him and said, "I heard you say, there was no man so far gone in London that Christ would not receive him. Did you mean it?" "Yes," he said. "Well," she says, "I found a man who said he was so bad that the Lord would not have anything to do with him. Will you go and see him?" He said, "I will be glad to go."

She took him to a brick building, in a narrow street, and he was on the fifth story. She said, "You had better go in alone." He went in and found a young man lying in the garret, on an old straw bed. He found he was very sick; and he whispered in his ear some kind words, and wanted to call his friends. The dying man said, "You are mistaken in the person." "Why so?" said Mr. Dawson. "I have no friends on earth," said the dying man. It is hard indeed, for a man to serve the devil, and come down to no friends. "Well," said he, "you have a friend in Christ," and he told him how Jesus loved and pitied him, and would save him. He read different portions of Scripture and prayed with the man.

After praying with him a long time, the light of the gospel began to break into his dark soul, and his heart went out toward those whom he had injured. He said, "If my father would only forgive me I could die happy."

"Who is your father?" He told him, and Mr. Dawson said, "I will go and see him." "No," the sick man said, "he has cast me off." But William Dawson knew he would receive him, so he got his father's address and said, "I will go."

He came to the west end of London, and rang the bell of the house where the father lived. A servant in livery came to the door, and Mr. Dawson asked if his master was in. The servant showed him in and told him to wait a few minutes. Presently the merchant came in. Mr. Dawson said to him, "You have a son by the name of Joseph." The merchant said, "No, sir; if you come to talk to me about that worthless vagabond, you shall leave the house; I have disinherited him." Mr. Dawson said, "He will not be your boy by night; but he will be as long as he lives." The man said, "Is my boy sick?" "Yes, he is dying. I do not ask you to help bury him, I will attend to that, but he wants you to forgive him, and then he will die in peace." The tears trickled down the father's cheeks. Said he, "Does Joseph want me to forgive him? I would have forgiven him long ago if I had known that."

In a few minutes he was in a carriage, and they went to the house where the boy was; and as they ascended the filthy stairs, he said, "Did you find my boy here? I would have taken him to my heart if I had known this." When his father came in the boy cried, "Can you forgive me all my past sins?" The father came over to the boy and bent over him, and kissed him, and said, "I would have forgiven you, long ago." And he said, "Let my servant put you in my carriage." The dying man said, "I am too sick; I can die happy now. I think God, for Christ's sake, has forgiven me." The prodigal told the father of the Savior's love; and then, his head lying upon his father's bosom, he breathed his last, and rose to heaven.

If your father or mother forsake you, the Lord Jesus Christ will not. Oh, may you press into the kingdom of heaven tonight, and while Mr. Sankey sings, "Oh, prodigal son, come home," I hope every one will come home. Oh, may hundreds come home while this is sung. Let us bow our heads while he sings it.

The Prodigal's Father

John Wilbur Chapman (1859-1918) was ordained a Presbyterian minister and served churches in Ohio, Indiana, New York and Pennsylvania. He was a pastor who did the work of an evangelist and was greatly blessed of God. He ministered with D.L. Moody and was associated for ten years with Charles Alexander, the well-known Christian musician. They made a world tour that resulted in thousands coming to Christ. Chapman was the first director of the Winona Lake (Indiana) Bible Conference, and also assisted the conferences at Montreat, North Carolina, and Stony Brook, Long Island, New York.

This sermon is taken from his book *"And Peter" and Other Sermons,* published in 1895 by the Bible Institute Colportage Association, Chicago.

J. Wilbur Chapman

3

THE PRODIGAL'S FATHER

But when he was yet a great way off, his father saw him
and had compassion and ran, and kissed him. . . . The
father said to his servants, Bring forth the best robe and
put it on him, and put a ring on his hand, and shoes on
his feet. And bring the fatted calf, and kill it (Luke 15:20-
23).

OF MAKING MANY sermons on the prodigal son, there
seems to be no end. Yet I was in the ministry fifteen
years before I preached from any part of the parable.
There may be many reasons why, as a rule, we turn
away from it. It may be that the picture is too realistic.

I was standing in the prison chapel at Joliet, Illinois,
when a request was made that I should conduct a
service for the convicts. Just as I was leaving the
building, the officer said to me, "By the way, if you
should come, do not preach on any part of the prodigal.
We have had twenty-four ministers here by actual
count, and every one of them gave us the prodigal son,
and these poor fellows have had about as much prodigal
as they can stand."

It may also be that we have turned away from the
story of the prodigal because it is such familiar ground
that it has lost its charm for us.

I was traveling by train through the magnificent
Rocky Mountains some time ago. When we had plunged
into the Royal Gorge, and later swung into the Grand
Canyon, it seemed to me that more awe-inspiring
scenery could not be found in all the world. It occurred
to me that if I had never been impressed before with
the existence of God, I should have cried out unto Him
in the midst of those mountain peaks.

I noticed that everyone in the car, with one single
exception, was gazing in rapt admiration. This one

woman was intently reading a book, and to my knowledge, she did not lift her eyes once from the printed page while we were in that wonderful scenery. When we had swung out into the great tableland, I overheard her say to a friend, "This is the thirteenth time I have crossed the mountains. The first time I could not keep the tears from rolling down my cheeks, so impressed was I, but now," she said, "I know it so well that I frequently go through the whole range with scarcely a glance cast out the window."

That is how it can be with us! We read God's Word, yet that which fills heaven with wonder and furnishes the angels a theme for never-ending praise, we read with indifference or fail to read at all. And yet my own confession is that I never had understood, until recently, the best of this story of the prodigal. As we look into this parable, let us not grow weary of its beauty and grandeur. Let us allow it to teach us in a new and vibrant way as we look at the role of the prodigal's father.

Did it ever occur to you that in the pictures of the fathers of the Bible you were always given a vision of one part of the nature of God? Jacob crying out, "Me have ye bereaved of my children; Joseph is not, and Simeon is not, and ye will take Benjamin away" (Gen. 42:36) is an illustration of God crying out in His great tenderness over the lost. David exclaiming, "Oh, Absalom, my son, my son! Would God I had died for thee" (2 Sam. 18:33), is just a hint of the way God feels over His own lost ones for whom His Son has died. And yet better than any picture of a father as the revelation of God is the life of Jesus, His Son, from whose lips we have heard these words, "He that hath seen me hath seen the Father" (John 14:9). As we put all these things together, and as we read again the story of the prodigal, our hearts burn within us as we see God.

But When He Was Yet a Great Way Off

These words must have a wonderful meaning, for the measurement of "a great way off" is from God's standpoint. It would be an awful thing to be "a great way off" according to man's conception, but when it is the computation of One who is infinite we are startled. Yet our amazement gives way instantly to adoration, for we are told that even if we are so great a distance from Him we are not to be discouraged. In Acts 2:39, we read that the promise of salvation goes to "all that are afar off," and in Ephesians 2, we are told that "ye who sometimes were far off are made nigh by the blood of Christ" (v. 13), and that Jesus Christ "came and preached peace to you which were afar off" (v. 17), as well as to them that were near. It never is any question with God as to how deeply one has sinned. It is a remarkable thing that throughout the whole Bible He has ever chosen the most conspicuous sins and the most flagrant sinners to demonstrate to us His willingness to forgive.

God requires but three things if we would know Him in this way.

First, there must be a willing mind. In Isaiah 1:19, we read, "If ye be willing and obedient, ye shall eat the good of the land." In another place we read, "if there be first a willing mind, it is accepted according to that which a man hath, and not according to that which he hath not" (2 Cor. 8:12). In still another place we are told, "If any man will do His will, he shall know of the doctrine" (John 7:17). God Himself, infinite though He may be, will not save us against our will.

Second, there must be a desire to know the truth and to do it. Mere knowledge of the truth may be our condemnation, and it is the saddest thing in the world that so many people know and yet are unwilling to do. It will be an awful judgment that must finally fall upon the rank and file of men because all their lives they lived under the shadow of the church and heard the preaching of the Word, all of which condemns them.

The third requirement is an honest confession of one's intentions. God never gives to a person more light than he uses. But if there is in the heart a single desire, however faint, to know Him, and that desire is confessed before men and unto God, He enlarges our vision and sheds upon us more abundant light. It is always by the way of confession that we enter into the fulness of joy.

His Father Saw Him

D.L. Moody says that the prodigal's father was looking through the telescope of his love. I have always felt that he was looking through his tears. It is said that when astronomers want to increase the scope of their vision they add to the number of lenses. Sometimes our falling tears are like the lenses in the telescope. They bring distant objects close to us.

What a comfort it is to know that the Great Father of us all looks after us with a pity that is infinite and with a sympathy that is beyond conception. The vision of the prodigal's father was limited, but God's eye sweeps through all space, and He sees us wherever we are. He can even behold our thoughts.

When you bowed your head during a gospel invitation and said, "I ought to come," and partly lifted your hand as an expression of your intention, or started to rise that you might make public your confession, He saw you and was ready to run to meet you. This is all that he requires on your part. He is ready to do all the rest.

It is said that William Rainsford of England, while speaking in one of the Northfield conferences, related the story of an old friend of his, a German professor who was an agnostic. As you know, the creed of the agnostic is simply, "I do not know." This old professor came to visit Dr. Rainsford and went with him to all the services of his church. When the day was ended the clergyman said to him, "Professor, tell me what you think of it all." His answer was, "It is beautiful, but that is all I can say." Then Dr. Rainsford put to him these questions:

First, "Do you not think that it is possible that there may be a God?" The old professor said, "Yes, possible."

Second, "Then do you not think that it is probable that God has made a revelation of Himself to His creatures?" His friend answered, "Yes, probable."

Third, "Well, do you not think," said he, "that He would make that revelation plain if we were to ask Him?" The old professor answered, "I should think He would be obliged to."

"Well," said Dr. Rainsford, "have you ever asked Him?" The old man answered, "No."

"For my sake," said he, "will you ask Him now?" They fell on their knees in the study, and the old minister said, "Lord God, reveal Thyself unto my dear friend." When his prayer was ended he said, "Now, Professor, you pray." The old man lifted his eyes and said, "Oh, God," and then as if he felt he had gone too far, he changed his petition, and said, "Oh, God, if there be a God, show me the light and I will ——" and he was just going on to say, "I will walk in it," when suddenly he sprang to his feet with his face radiant and shouted, "Why, I see it, I see it, and it is glorious!" His agnosticism took wings and departed from him. Faith filled his heart and joy thrilled in his soul. He has from that time to this been a good disciple of Jesus Christ. In the light of all this I made the plea: Encourage your least desire, and you shall come to know Him whom to know is life eternal.

He Had Compassion and Ran

I never knew until recently what the word *compassion* meant. I know now that it indicates one's suffering with another. It is this that makes the story of a man's transgression so pathetic. Other hearts are made to ache and almost break. Other eyes are filled with tears and other lives made desolate. I can see this old father going up to the outlook from his home, gazing off in the direction which his boy had taken, coming down the steps again like David of old crying out, "Oh, my son, my son, would God I had died for you!" (2 Sam. 18:33). He had compassion.

We had in our city a young man who was more than ordinarily prosperous in his business, and his prosperity seemed to be the cause of his downfall. It became so obvious that his partners called him into their office to say that he must either mend his ways or dispose of his interests in the concern. His promises were good, and all went well for a little while. But then the failure became worse than ever, and his partners insisted that he should dispose of his interests to them. He began to lose money rapidly. He went from bad to worse until not long ago they found him floating in the river, for he had taken his own life.

The story is sad in the extreme, but the saddest portion of it is found in the fact that there is an old man today going about the streets of the city mourning for his son. He scarcely lifts his eyes from the ground as he walks. Sometimes you behold him with the tears rolling down his cheeks. He has compassion.

Now think of God's compassion. We can never sin, breaking even the least of God's commandments, that the heart of the great and loving Father does not yearn over him and long for his return.

What Did He Do?

We all know this story so thoroughly that it would seem almost unnecessary to emphasize what the father did when he and his son met. But for the sake of the story let me say this:

First, "he kissed him." You will notice that he did not wait until the boy's garments had been changed or the signs of his wanderings removed. There would have been no grace in this. But with his son clad in all his rags, the father threw his arms around him, drew him close against his heart, and gave him the kiss that was the sign of complete reconciliation.

This reconciliation is what Jesus Christ waits to give to every wandering soul. The old hymn says, "My God is reconciled," and this is the teaching of the Scriptures. It is not necessary that I should work myself up into a fever of excitement, nor weep and wail in the depths of my despair, but it is necessary only that I should receive what God offers me in Jesus Christ. The first step in the Christian life is an acceptance of that which comes from above.

We had in Philadelphia a young man belonging to one of the so-called "better families," who by his wayward actions disgraced his father and finally broke his heart. After a little while, he left his home, went to Baltimore and then on to Washington. After months of wandering, he decided to return. He was ashamed to meet the members of his family, but he knew that if he made a certain peculiar sound at the door at midnight there was one who would hear and understand. When he stood before that door, it was swung open and without a word of reproach his mother bade him welcome.

The next morning he did not come down from his room, and on the second morning he was ashamed to come. But on the third morning, as he descended the stairway, his brother, a physician, met him and said, "Edward, mother is dying." She had been suddenly stricken down and was anxious to see him. He made his way into her room, knelt beside her bed, and sobbed out, "Oh, Mother, I beseech you forgive me!" With her last departing strength she drew close to him, placed her lips close to his ear, and said, "My dear boy, I would have forgiven you long ago if you had only accepted it." This is a picture of God. With a love that is infinite and a pity beyond description, He waits to save everyone who will but simply receive His gift of life.

Second, I have always imagined that when the father started out from the house running to meet his boy, that the servants must have noticed him, and possibly they ran after him. When the father saw the condition of the son, I can hear him as he turned to the approaching servants to say, "Run, bring the best robe and put it on him;" and it is a beautiful thing to me to know that when they brought the robe the father wrapped it round about him, thus covering over all the signs of his wanderings. This is what God does for you and for me. The moment we believe, the robe of Christ's righteousness is placed about us, and God looks upon us as without spot or blemish, for we are at once accepted in the beloved.

I remember that when Jonathan was dead and David wanted to do something for someone who belonged to him, the only person he could find was poor, little, lame Mephibosheth. He was lame on both his feet, you will remember (his nurse had dropped him as she was fleeing away from the enemy), but when David found him he placed him at the king's table and in such a position that his lameness was hidden. If you had been on the opposite side from his you never would have known that he had a mark of deformity about him. This is what God does for every poor, wandering, lost one that comes to Him! "I, even I, am He who blotteth out thy transgressions, . . . and I will not remember thy sins" (Isa. 43:25).

Third, he put the ring on his hand. The ring is always the emblem for completeness. And this was a beautiful illustration of the fact that the father's love was perfect, and that his love had not been affected by the wanderings of the boy. This is certainly true of God, and I know of no better object to portray His love than a ring.

"For the love of God is broader than the measure of man's mind, And the heart of the Eternal is most wonderfully kind."

Fourth, he put shoes on his feet. I can see the poor boy as he hobbles on to meet his father, his feet bleeding at every step. The shoes were tattered and he walked with difficulty. But later, when he was well shod with shoes from the king's house, I can see him taking the hand of the old father and running back to his home. One of the most common excuses people give for not yielding to Christ is the fear that they may not hold out. That's why it is comforting to know that the moment we are saved He puts shoes on our feet and that we are shod with the preparation of the gospel of peace.

Ira Sankey told the story of his young son who was with him in Scotland when he wore for the first time what in that country is known as a top coat. They were walking out one cold day, and the way was slippery.

The little fellow's hands were deep down in his pockets. His father said to him, "My son, you had better let me take your hand." But, Sankey said, "You never could persuade a boy with a new top coat to take his hands from his pockets." They reached a slippery place, and the boy had a hard fall. Then his pride began to depart, and he said, "I will take your hand," and he reached up and clasped his father's hand the best he could. When a second slippery place was reached, the clasp was broken and the second fall was harder than the first. Now all his pride was gone. Raising his little hand he said, "You may take it now." Continuing the story, Sankey said, "I clasped it round about with my great hand and we continued our walk; and when we reached the slippery places, the little feet would start to go and I would hold him up."

This is a picture for the Christian. I am saved not so much because I have hold of God as because *God has hold of me*. He not only gives me shoes with which I may walk and which never wear out, but Christ holds my hand in His. I shall never perish, neither shall any man pluck me out of His hand. His Father is greater, and no man shall ever pluck me out of His Father's hand; and so between the hand of God and the hand of Christ I am secure.

And They Killed for Him the Fatted Calf

I can see the old father as he runs from home to home exclaiming, "Come in and rejoice with me, for my boy was dead and is alive again. He was lost and is found," and they begin to be merry. One can never have the fatted calf killed for him but once, but one of the delightful things about the Christian life is that we may repeatedly sit down to enjoy the feast for others, and it is thrilling to know that we never have a time of feasting here that they do not have a time of rejoicing in heaven. "There is joy in the presence of the angels of God over one sinner that repenteth" (Luke 15:10).

At the close of a meeting in Joliet, Illinois, I sat down with evangelist, H. W. Brown, and he told me this story.

A number of years before, he had a remarkable work of grace in the lake region of Wisconsin in that town of the strange name, Oconomowoc. After his work of grace, he returned one day for a little visit. As he stepped off the train, he saw at the station an old man named James Stewart. Knowing him well, he asked him why he was there. The old man replied that his boy had gone away from home, saying, "Father, I will return some day, but I can not tell when." Mr. Stewart said, "I am waiting for him to come back." Strange as it may seem, thirteen years later he revisited that old town, and the first man he saw when getting off the train was this old father. Rev. Brown had forgotten his story, but the old man met him, saying, "Mr. Brown, he hasn't come yet, but he will come, and I am waiting."

"Just then," said my friend, "I lifted up my eyes and saw a young man walking down the aisle of the car. I said to myself, If I was not sure that the boy was dead, I would say that that was the son." But other eyes had seen him too, and with a great bound the old father sprang to the steps of the car. When the boy reached the platform, in less time than I can tell it, he was in his father's arms. The old father sobbed out, "Oh, my son, thank God, you've come, you've come." Then, turning to my friend, he said, "Mr. Brown, I should have waited until I died." Thus God waits, and looks and yearns and loves. Thus Jesus Christ entreats us to look unto Him and be saved, and in His name I bid you come.

> Thy sins I bore on Calvary's tree,
> The stripes, thy due, were laid on me,
> That peace and pardon might be free,
> Oh, weary sinner, come!
>
> Go leave thy burden at the cross,
> Count all thy gains but empty dross,
> My grace repays all earthly loss,
> Oh, needy sinner, come!

NOTES

Gifts to the Prodigal

Alexander Maclaren (1826-1910) was one of Great Britain's most famous preachers. While pastoring the Union Chapel, Manchester (1858-1903), he became known as "the prince of expository preachers." Rarely active in denominational or civic affairs, Maclaren invested his time studying the Word in the original and sharing its truths with others in sermons that are still models of effective expository preaching. He published a number of books of sermons and climaxed his ministry by publishing his monumental *Expositions of Holy Scripture.*

Alexander Maclaren

4

GIFTS TO THE PRODIGAL

... Bring forth the best robe, and put it on him; and put a ring on his hand, and shoes on his feet. And bring the fatted calf, and kill it... (Luke 15:22, 23).

GOD'S GIVING ALWAYS follows His forgiving. It is not so with us. We think ourselves very magnanimous when we pardon; and we seldom go on to lavish favors where we have overlooked faults. Perhaps it is right that men who have offended against men should earn restoration by acts, and should have to ride quarantine, as it were, for a time. But I question whether forgiveness is ever true which is not, like God's, attended by large-hearted gifts.

If pardon is only the non-infliction of penalty, then it is natural enough that it should be considered sufficient by itself, and that the evildoer should not be rewarded for having been bad. But if pardon is the outflow of the love of the offender, then it can scarcely be content with simply giving the debtor his discharge and turning him into the world penniless.

Whatever pardon may mean among men, God's forgiveness is essentially the communication of His love to us sinners, as if we had never sinned at all. And that being so, that love cannot stop working until it has given all it can bestow or we can receive. God does not do things by halves, and *He always gives when He forgives.*

That is the great truth of the last part of this immortal parable. And it is one of the points in which it differs from, and towers high above, the two preceding ones. The lost sheep was carried back to the pastures and turned loose there. Needing no further special care, it began to nibble as if nothing had happened. The last drachma was simply put back in the woman's purse.

But the lost son was pardoned. Being pardoned, he was capable of receiving greater gifts than he has before. These gifts are remarkably detailed in the words of our text.

Now, of course, it is always risky to seek a spiritual interpretation of every point in a parable. Many of the points are mere drapery. On the other hand, we may very easily fall into the error of treating as insignificant these details that really are meant to be full of instruction. And I cannot help thinking—although many would differ from me—that this detailed enumeration of the gifts to the prodigal is meant to be translated into the terms of spiritual experience. So I desire to look at them as suggesting for us the gifts of God that accompany forgiveness. I take the catalogue as it stands—the Robe, the Ring, the Shoes, the Feast.

The Robe

"Bring forth the best robe, and put it on him." That was the command. This detail, of course, like all the others, refers back to, and casts light upon, the supposed condition of the spendthrift when he came back. There he stood, with the stain of travel and the stench of the pig-sty on his ragged garments. No doubt he was wearing the remains of the tawdry finery he had worn in the world—winespots and stains and filth of all sorts were on the rags. The father says, "Take them all off him, and put the best robe upon him." What does that mean?

Well, we all know the familiar metaphor by which qualities of mind and traits of character are described as being the dress of the spirit. We talk about being "arrayed in purity," "clad in zeal" (Isa. 59:17), "clothed with humility" (1 Peter 5:5), "girded with power" (Ps. 65:6), and so on. If we turn to Scripture, we find running through it a whole series of instances of this metaphor, which guide us at once to its true meaning. Zechariah saw in vision the high priest standing at the heavenly tribunal, clad in filthy garments. A voice said, "Take away the filthy garments from him," and the interpretation is added: "Behold! I have caused thine iniquity to pass from thee, and I will clothe thee with a change of raiment" (3:4).

You remember our Lord's parable of the man with a wedding garment. You remember the apostle Paul's frequent use of the metaphor of "putting off the old man, putting on the new." You remember, finally, the visions of the last days, in which the seer in Patmos saw the armies in heaven that followed their victorious Commander, "arrayed in fine linen, clean and white; for the fine linen is the righteousness of the saints" (Rev. 19:8).

If we put all these together, surely I am not forcing a meaning on a nonsignificant detail when I say that here we have shadowed for us this great thought: The result of the divine forgiveness coming upon a man is that he is clothed with a character that makes him fit to sit down at his Father's table. They tell us that forgiveness is impossible, because things done must have their consequences, and that character is the slow formation of actions, precipitated, as it were, from our deeds. That is all true. But it does not conflict with this other truth that there may and does comes into men's hearts, when they set their faith on Jesus Christ, a new power that transforms the nature and causes old things to pass away.

God's forgiveness revolutionizes a life. Similar effects follow even human pardons for small offenses. Brute natures are held in by penalties, and to them pardon means impunity, and impunity means license, and license means lust. But wherever there is a heart with love to the offended in it, there is nothing that will so fill it with loathing of its past self as the assurance that free forgiveness has come. Is it the rod or the mother's kiss that makes a child hate his sin most? Lift up your thoughts to God, and think how He, up there in the heavens bends over you in frank, free forgiveness. Surely that, more than all punishments or threatenings of terrors, will cause you to turn away from evil and to loathe the sins that have been forgiven.

Ezekiel went very deep when he said, "Thou mayest remember and be confounded, and never open thy mouth any more because of the shame, when I am pacified toward thee for all that thou hast done, saith the Lord God" (Ezek. 16:63).

But that is not all. Given alone with forgiveness, and wrapped up in it, is a new power, one that makes all things new and changes a man. It would be a poor gospel for me to stand up and preach if all I had to proclaim to men was the divine forgiveness and that hell's door was barred and some outward heaven was flung open. But the true gospel offers forgiveness as preliminary to the bestowal of the highest gifts of God. The pardoned man is stripped of his rags and clothed with a new nature, which God Himself bestows.

That is what we all need. We have not all been in the pig-sty; we have not all fallen into gross sin. But we *have* all turned our backs on our Father; we *have* all wanted to be independent; we *have* all preferred the far-off land to being near home. And, dear brethren, the character that you have made for yourselves clings to you like the poisoned Nessus' shirt to Hercules. You cannot strip it off. You may get part of it away, but you cannot entirely cast it from your limbs, nor free yourself from the entanglements of its tatters. Go to God, and He will smile away your sin. His forgiving love will melt the stains and the evil, as the sun this morning drank up the mists. They who come to Him, knowing themselves to be foul and needing forgiveness, will surely receive from Him "the fine linen white and pure, the righteousness of saints" (Rev. 19:8).

The Ring

This prodigal lad only wanted to be placed in the position of a slave, but his father said, "Put a ring on his hand" (Luke 15:22). The ring is an emblem of wealth, position, honor; that is one meaning of this gift to the penitent. Still further, it is an ornament to the hand on which it glistens. It is a sign of delegated authority and of representative character—as when

Joseph was exalted to be the second man in Egypt, and Pharaoh's signet-ring was plucked off and placed on his finger (Gen. 41:42). All these thoughts are, it seems to me, clustered in, and fairly deducible from, this one detail.

Freedom, exaltation, dignity of position are expressed. And that opens up a thought that needs to be set forth carefully and reservedly. Yet it is, still true: By the mercy and miraculous lovingkindness and quickening power of God in the gospel, it is possible that the lower a man falls the higher he may rise. I know, of course, that it is better to be innocent than to be cleansed. I know, and every man that looks into his own heart knows, that forgiven sins may leave scars; that the memory may be loaded with many a foul and painful remembrance; that the fetters may be stricken off the limbs, but the marks of them, and the way of walking that they compelled, may persist long after deliverance. But I know, too, that redeemed men are higher in final position than angels that never fell. And I know that, though it is too much to say that the greater the sinner the greater the saint, it still remains true the sin repented and forgiven may be, as it were, an elevation upon which a man may stand to reach higher than, apparently, he otherwise would reach in the divine life.

Of course, I do not say to anyone, "Try it." Indeed, the poorest of us has sins enough to get all the benefit out of repentance and forgiveness. Yet, if there is any man here—and I hope there is—saying to himself, "I have got too low down ever to master this, that, or the other evil; I have stained myself so foully that I cannot hope to have the black marks erased," I say to him, "Remember that the man who ended with a ring on his finger, honored and dignified, was the man that had herded with pigs, and stank, and all but rotted with his fleshly crimes."

Therefore, nobody need doubt but that for him, however low he has gone, and however far he has gone, there is restoration possible to a higher dignity than the pure spirits that never transgressed at any time

God's commandment will ever attain. He who has within himself the experience of repentance, of pardon, and who has come into living contact with Jesus Christ as Redeemer, can teach angels how blessed it is to be a child of God.

Not any less distinctly are the other two things that I have referred to brought out in this metaphor. Not only is the ring the sign of dignity, but it is also the sign of delegated authority and representative character. God sets poor penitents to be His witnesses in His world, and to do His work here. A ring is an ornament to the hand that wears it, which means that where God gives pardon, He gives a strange beauty of character, one that a person can attain if he is true to himself and to his Redeemer. There should be no lives so lovely, none that flash with so many jeweled colors, as the lives of the men and women who have learned what it is to be miserable, what it is to repent, and what it is to be forgiven. So, though our "hands are full of blood" (Isa. 1:15), as the prophet says, though they have dabbled in all manner of pollution, though they have been the ready instruments of many evil things, we may all hope that, cleansed and whitened, even our hands will not lack the luster of that adornment which the loving father clasped upon the fingers of his penitent boy.

Shoes on His Feet

No doubt the prodigal had come back barefooted and filthy and bleeding, so it was important for the "keeping" of the narrative that this detail should appear. But I think it is something more than drapery.

Does it not speak to us of equipment for the walk of life? God *does* prepare men for future service, and for every step that they have to take, by giving to them His forgiveness for all that is past. The sense of the divine pardon will in itself fit a man, as nothing else will, for running with patience the race that is set before him. God does communicate, along with His forgiveness, to every one who seeks it, actual power to travel on life's common way in cheerful godliness. And he causes his feet to be "shod with the preparation of the gospel of peace" (Eph. 6:15).

Ah, brethren, life is a rough road for us all. But for those whose faces are set toward duty, God, and self-denial, it is especially so, though there are many compensating circumstances. There are places where sharp flints stick up in the path and cut the feet. There are places where rocks jut out for us to stumble over. There are all the trials and sorrows that necessarily attend upon our daily lives, trials that sometimes make us feel as if we had to walk across heated ploughshares, and every step was a separate agony. God will give us, if we go to Him for pardon, that which will defend us against the pains and the sorrows of life. The bare foot is cut by that which the shod foot tramples upon unconsciously.

There are foul places on all our paths, over which, when we pass, if we have nothing but our own naked selves, we shall certainly be defiled. God will give to the penitent man, if he will have it, that which will keep his feet from soil, even when they walk amidst filth. And if at any time some mud should stain the foot, and he that is washed needs again to wash his feet, the Master, with the towel and the basin, will not be far away.

There are enemies and dangers in life. A very important part of the equipment of the soldier in antiquity was the heavy boot, which enabled him to stand fast and resist the rush of the enemy. God will give to the penitent man, if he will have it, that which will set his foot upon a rock, "and establish [his] goings" (Ps. 40:2), and which will make him "able to withstand in the evil day, and having done all, to stand" (Eph. 6:13).

Brethren, defense, stability, shielding from pains, and protection against evil are all included in this great promise, which each of us can—if we will—realize for ourselves.

The Feast

The feast comes into view in the parable mainly to teach us the great truth that heaven keeps holiday, even when some poor waif comes shrinking back to his Father. But I do not touch upon that truth now, though it is the main significance of this last part of the story.

The prodigal was half starving, and the fatted calf was killed "for him," as his ill-conditioned brother grumbled (Luke 15:30). Remember what it was that drove him back—not his heart, nor his conscience, but his stomach. He did not desire to go back because dormant affection for his brother woke up or because a sense that he had been wrong stirred in him. He returned because he was hungry. And well he might be, when "the husks that the swine did eat" (Luke 15:16), were luxuries beyond his reach. Thank God for the teaching that even so low a motive as that is accepted by God; and that, if a man goes back, even for no better reason—as long as he does go back—he will be welcomed by the Father.

This poor boy was quite content to sink his sonship for the sake of a loaf, and all that he wanted was to relieve his hunger. So he had to learn that he could not get bread on his terms, and that what he wished most was not what he needed first. He has to be forgiven and bathed in the outflow of his father's love before he could be fed. And, being thus received, he could not fail to be fed. So the message for us is, first, forgiveness, and then every hunger of the heart satisfied; all desires met; every needful nourishment communicated, and the true bread ours for ever, if we choose to eat. "The meek shall eat and be satisfied" (Ps. 22:26).

I need not draw the picture—that picture of which there are many originals sitting in these pews before me—of the men that go forever roaming with a hungry heart. They travel through all the regions of life separate from God. Whether they seek their nourishment in the garbage of the sty, or whether fastidiously they look for it in the higher nutriment of mind and intellect and heart, they are still condemned to be unfilled.

Brethren, "Why do you spend your money for that . . . which satisfies not?" (Isa. 55:2). Here is the true way for all desires to be appeased. Go to God in Jesus Christ for forgiveness and then everything that you need shall be yours. "I counsel thee to buy of Me . . . white raiment that thou mayest be clothed" (Rev. 3:18). "He that eateth of this bread shall live for ever" (John 6:58).

A Young Man's Mind

Alexander Whyte (1836-1921) was known as "the last of the Puritans," and certainly his sermons were surgical as he magnified the glory of God and exposed the sinfulness of sin. He succeeded the noted Robert S. Candlish as pastor of free St. George's and reigned from that influential Edinburgh pulpit for nearly forty years. He loved to "dig again in the old wells" and share with his people truths learned from the devotional masters of the past. His evening Bible courses attracted the young people and led many into a deeper walk with God.

This sermon is taken from Whyte's *Bible Characters, Our Lord's Characters*, published in London in 1902 by Oliphant, Anderson and Faber, and included in *Bible Characters From the Old and New Testaments*, to be reprinted in 1990 by Kregel Publications.

5

A YOUNG MAN'S MIND

A certain man had two sons. And the younger of them said to his father, Father, give me the portion of goods that falleth to me. And he divided unto them his living. And not many days after, the younger son gathered all together, and took his journey into a far country, and there wasted his substance with riotous living (Luke 15:11-13).

THE COUNTRY-BRED BOY had been told seductive stories about the delights of city life. "A young man with a little money," he had been told, "can command anything he likes in the great city. A young man who has never been away from home can have no idea of the pleasures that are provided in the city for young men whose fathers have money. The games, the shows, the theaters, the circuses, the feasts, the dances, the freedom of all kinds; there is absolutely nothing that a young man's heart can desire that is not open to him who brings a good purse of money to the city with him."

All these intoxications were poured into this young man's imagination, and he was too good a pupil to ignore such instructions.

How long will my father live? he began to ask himself. How long will that old man continue to stand in my way? It is not reasonable that what really belongs to a young man should be kept from him so long. It is not fair to treat a grown-up man as if he were still a child. "Father, give me the portion of goods that falleth to me." It was a heartless speech. But secret visions of sin will soon harden the tenderest heart in the world.

Cogitatio et imaginatio, according to Thomas à Kempis, are the two first steps of a young man's heart on its way down to the pit. Keep a young man's thoughts and imaginations clean, and he is safe and will be a good son. But once polluted, by bad books or bad companionships, a young man's mind and imagination, and nothing in this world will hold that young man back from perdition.

A Far Country

Not many days later, the younger son gathered all together, took his journey into a far country, and there wasted his substance with riotous living. Let one who lived for a long time in that far country describe it. "A darkened heart is the far country. For it is not by our feet, but by our affections, that we either leave Thee or return to Thee. Nor did that younger son look out for chariots, or ships, or fly with visible wings, that he might go to the far country. Unclean affections, and a God-abandoned heart, that is the far country. This was the world at whose gate I lay in imagination, while yet a boy. And this was the abyss of my vileness when I was cast away from before Thine eyes. Who was so vile before Thee as I was? I was vile even to myself."

"And when he has spent all, there arose a mighty famine in that land; and he began to be in want" (Luke 15:14). *A mighty famine* is perfect English. It is one of those great strokes of translation that sometimes surpass the original. *A mighty famine* puts a perfect picture of that far country before us. Now what chance, in the midst of a mighty famine, had a prodigal son who had already wasted all his substance with riotous living? What hope was there for him? What could a penniless spendthrift do?

When he was covered with rags, and with all his bones staring till they could be counted, he threw himself upon a citizen of that country, and said, "Only give me one crust of bread and water, and I will do anything you like to command me. I have a father at home, but that is far away. Oh, for my father's sake, and he will repay you, give me something to eat." The citizen sent him into his fields to feed swine (15:15). "If I could see a boy of good make and mind, with the tokens on him of a refined nature, cast upon the world without provision, unable to say where he came from, or who were his family connections, I would conclude there was some secret connected with his history, and that he was one of whom, from one cause or another, his parents were ashamed." Such is one man's conception of the human race, as it is fallen away from God and gone into a far country.

And When He Came to Himself

Underline those words. Print them in capitals. Engrave them in letters of gold. "He came to himself." Up till now sin has abounded, but henceforth grace is much more to abound. And already the abounding grace that the prodigal son is so soon to be met with, is beginning to drop from the lips of the One who here tells the prodigal's sad story. Look at the beautiful way in which the terrible truth is softened in the telling. Every word is so tenderly, and almost apologetically, chosen.

You do not upbraid a son of yours when he is brought home to you safe and sound from the asylum. Whatever he may have said or done during his illness there, you refuse to listen to it. You say, My poor possessed child! You say, My son at that time was not responsible. And you shut your ears to all the heartless tales they tell about what he said and what he did when he was still beside himself. You rebuke his cruel accusers. You tell them that nobody reckons to a recovered man the things that would be reckoned and punished to an entirely sound-minded man.

These grace-chosen words, "When he came to himself," already prepare us for the speedy return and complete restoration of this unhappy son, whose infirmity and affliction, rather than his sin and guilt, are the subject of his history as it is here told to us.

"But when he was yet a great way off, his father saw him" (15:20). And we see him. Our Lord sees him, and He makes us see him. Look at him! Look how he runs! He runs like a man running for his life. He forgets his bleeding feet and his hungry belly. He outstrips everybody on the same road. He runs as he never ran before. But when he comes to the first sight of his father's house his strength suddenly fails him. He stands still, he sinks down, he beats his breast. He cries out as with an intolerable pain till the passersby hasten on in fear. The man is possessed, one says to him. How long will you be drunk? says another. But he sees them not. He hears them not. The only things he sees is his father's house through his tears and his sobs. And all that any of the people in the fields or on the road could make out from him was always this: "Against thee, thee only, have I sinned, and done this evil in thy sight!"

And, then, all this long far-country time, his father's gray hairs were being brought down with sorrow to the grave. His father had never been the same man since that evil day when his son had left his father's door without kissing his father. Ever since that day, he had walked up and down his house a broken-hearted man. His very reapers had wept for him as they saw him walking up and down alone in his harvest fields. Every night he sat and looked out of his window till the darkness fell again on all the land. And all night through the darkness he listened for a footstep that never came. But, at last one day! That is none other than my long-lost son! And "when he was yet a great way off, his father saw him, and had compassion, and ran, and fell on his neck, and kissed him" (15:20).

The Danger of Evil Influence

And now, among many other things, our Lord, I feel sure, would have us learn from this family history such things as this—*The unspeakable evil of a mind early stained with the images of sensual sin.* This young man was at one time as innocent of this sin, and was as loyal to his father and mother, as are any of your sons or mine. But on a fatal day, some bad man told him a bad story. Someone whispered to his heart some of the evil secrets of Satan's kingdom. And then there was first the sinful knowledge. Next there arose out of that a sinful imagination, a picture of the sin, and then the young sinner's heart took a secret delight in the knowledge and the vision. Finally he sought for an opportunity, and the opportunity soon came. A bad companion will do it. A bad book will do it. A bad picture will do it. The very classics themselves will sometimes do it.

It is being done every day in our workshops, and in our schools, and in our colleges. A bad story will do it. A bad song will do it. A bad jest will do it. Indeed, it is in the very air that all our sons breathe. It is in the very bread they eat. It is in the very water they drink. They cannot be in this world and clean escape it.

For myself, one of the saintliest men I ever knew once told me certain evil things, just out of the evil fulness of his heart, when I was not asking for them. Evil things that I would not have known to this day but for that conversation. Supply me with a knife deep enough and sharp enough to cut that corrupt spot out of my memory, and I will from this moment, cast it out on the dunghill of the devil forever—as we had, at last, to cut off and cast him. It was someone like my early friend who polluted that young man's imagination till nothing could keep him back from becoming the prodigal son of whom our Lord here tells us all these things for our warning and for our rebuke.

The Father's Compassion

The very finest point in all this history full of fine points, is this, "When he was a great way off, his father saw him, and had compassion on him." There is nothing more true in our own history than just this, and nothing more blessed for us to be told than just this, that our Father also sees us when we are yet a great way off from Him, and has compassion on us. When we are just beginning to remember that we have a Father; when we are just beginning to repent toward Him; when we are just beginning to pray to Him; when we are just beginning to believe on Him, and on His Son

Jesus Christ our Savior; when we are still at the very first beginnings of a penitent, returning, obedient, pure, and godly, life; yes, when we are yet a great way off from all these things, our Father sees us, and has compassion on us, and comes to meet us. I do not know a sweeter or a more consoling scripture anywhere than this, "When he was yet a great way off." What grace is in that! What encouragement, what hope, what comfort, what life from the dead is in that! Blessed be the lips that told this whole incomparable story, and added to it these words of gold: "a great way off."

Final Observations

This whole story, in every syllable of it, has its exact and complete fulfillment in ourselves every day. One preacher—prince of Scripture exposition—is unsure whether our Lord intended this family story to set forth the first conversion of a great sinner or the repeated restorations of a great backslider. I think our Lord intended to set forth both, and much more than both. For not one, nor two, nor three, but all the steps and all the stages of sin and salvation in the soul of man are most impressively and most unmistakably set before us in this masterpiece of our Master. From the temptation and fall of Adam, on to the marriage supper of the Lamb—all the history of the Church of God, and all the experiences of the individual sinner and saint, are to be found set forth in this most wonderful of all our Lord's histories.

John Howe warns us that we must not think it strange if all the requisites to our salvation are not to be found together in any single passage of Holy Scripture. But, on the other hand, I will take it upon myself to say that all the incidents and all the experiences of this evangelical history are to be found together in every soul of man who is under a full and perfect salvation. In a well-told story like this, all that the prodigal son came through, from first to last, must of necessity be set forth in so many successive steps and stages: the one step and stage following on the other. But that is not at all the case in the actual life of sin and grace in the soul. The soul is such that it is passing through *all* the steps and *all* the stages of sin and salvation at one and the same time. Some of the steps and stages of sin and salvation may be more present and more pressing at one time than at another time, but they are all somewhere or other within the soul, and are ready to spring up in it.

We speak in our shallow way about the apostle Paul being forever out of the seventh of the Romans and forever into the eighth. But Paul never spoke in the superficial fashion about himself. And he could not. For both chapters were fulfilling themselves within their profound author: sometimes at one and the same moment. Sometimes the old man was uppermost in Paul, and sometimes the new man; sometimes the flesh, and sometimes the spirit; sometimes the law and sin and death had Paul under their feet, and sometimes he was more than a conqueror over all the three. But all the time, all the three were within Paul. Every page he writes and every sermon he preaches, shows it. And so it is with ourselves, so far as this history, and so far as Paul's history, is our history.

Like the prodigal son, we are always having lewd stories told us about the far country. We are always dreaming of being at liberty to do as we like. We are always receiving our portion of goods, and we are always wasting our substance. We are always trying in vain to fill our belly with the husks that the swine do eat. And we are always arising and returning to our Father's house. In endless ways, impossible to be told, but by all God's true children every day to be experienced, every step and every stage of the prodigal's experience, both before he came to himself, and after it, is all to be found in the manifold, boundless, all-embracing, experience of every truly gracious heart.

In His unsearchable wisdom, God has set both the whole world of sin, and the whole world of salvation, in every truly renewed heart. And that is not done in successive and surmounting steps and stages, but at one and the same time. And that accumulating, complex, and exquisitely painful state of things will go on in every truly regenerate heart till that day dawns when the greatest prodigal of us all, and the saddest saint of us all, shall begin to be merry.

NOTES

The Prodigal Son

Joseph Parker (1830-1902) was one of England's most popular preachers. Largely self-educated, Parker had pulpit gifts that soon moved him into leadership among the Congregationalists. He was a fearless and imaginative preacher who attracted both common people and the aristocracy, and he was particularly a "man's preacher." His *People Bible* is a collection of the shorthand reports of the sermons and prayers Parker delivered as he preached through the entire Bible in seven years (1884-91). He pastored the Poultry Church, London, later called The City Temple, from 1869 until his death.

This sermon is taken from volume 20 of *The People's Bible* (London: Hazell, Watson and Viney, 1900).

Joseph Parker

6

THE PRODIGAL SON

A certain man had two sons. And the younger of them
said to his father, Father, give me the portion of goods
that falleth to me. And he divided unto them his living
(Luke 15:11, 12).

THE MAN WAS a man of substance. It may be a fortunate
or an unfortunate circumstance, as events may prove.
There is nothing wrong in being a substantial man in
society; yet having great riches may be one of the
greatest calamities that ever occurred in a man's life.

The younger son did not say, "Father, I am tired of a
lazy life, and now I am determined to do something for
my own bread. I have been turning over this great
problem of life in my mind, and I find that life is a
responsibility, life is a discipline, and although I have
been born under circumstances of conspicuous
advantage, I think it right to go out and do something
to make my own position, to establish my own title, to
be called and to be treated as a man." What did the
young man say? He said, "Father, I am a youth of
fortune; please give to me the portion of goods that
falleth to me." He had been scheming, it appears, but
scheming in a wrong direction. He had been *scheming
in the direction of self-enjoyment;* he was going out to
taste the sweets of liberty; the time had come, in his
consciousness, when he thought that he would enjoy a
little more freedom, and the first notion that occurred
to him was to get clear of his father.

Many a man has had precisely the same lucky
suggestion present to his mind by the great enemy.
The father has stood in the way; the father's old-world
notions have been impediments in the path of supposed
progress and enjoyment and liberty; and the young
man's great concern has been to get rid of his own

father! It looks well. "Let me open a door in my father's house, go into the wide world with the portion of goods that falleth to me, and all will be sunshine and beauty, music and rest." It is evident that the young man was *not a man of robust understanding;* yet he was not to be blamed for having had very little experience of the world. He thought that life would be enjoyable if only he had liberty. I propose now to follow him in his journeyings, to see what his experience was, to collect it for the advantage of all who need a moral exhortation upon this point, and to inquire at last whether there cannot be some better way of spending the days that God has put into our keeping as a trust.

Why a Far Country?

The young man gathered all together, took his journey into a far country, thinking that the farther from home the sweeter and larger would be the liberty. I fear he has planned something in his heart— *something he would not like to do just within the neighborhood of his own father's house.* If not, he gave way to the sophism which exercises a very malign influence upon a good many of us, namely this: *That we must go a long way off in order to be blest, not knowing that the true blessing grows just at arm's length,* forgetting that the fountain of the truest joy springs within us and not outside of us. Yet how many there are who travel mile after mile to get joy, to secure rest. They forget that they might have it without going out of themselves, except in so far as they go into God and truth and purity!

Wasting Everything

The young man has gone. And a merry day he has of it at first. His pockets are full, he has health on his side, many a pleasant memory sings to him, he has not yet tasted of the bitterness of life. It would be cruel if a man who is going to serve the devil could not have just a few hours of introductory enjoyment, or something that he at least mistakes for delight. A man cannot cut off good ties all in a moment; the ligaments require some time to get thoroughly through; and while the spell of old memories and traditions is upon the man, he imagines that he is going out into a large and wealthy place, and that every step he takes is a step in the direction of comfort and honor. When he got into the far country what did he do? He wasted his substance in riotous living; stepped out of liberty into license. At one bound he seems to have cleared the region of discipline and entered into the sphere of licentiousness. He wasted his substance.

There is nothing so easy as waste. It does not require any genius to waste property, to waste beauty, to waste life. Any man can waste what he has. It is easy to do the destructive part of life's work; the difficulty is to gather, to accumulate, to amass, and yet to hold all that has been brought together in the right spirit, and to administer it to the right ends.

Why did he show such bad skill? How does it come that in a moment he was master of the art of wasting? Because he has never mastered the art of earning his own living. Everything had been provided for him. When he came down to breakfast—toward 10, the family hour being 7 in the morning—he found the things still waiting for him, and at dinner he found the table lavishly spread without his having worked for a single morsel of food that was upon the board. When he was sick, the physician was within call. And when he felt any desire to please himself, his father and his mother were but too ready to gratify his desires.

Now the young fool goes out into the world to find his joy in wasting, destroying, trampling under foot all the things that he has got! And what blame? We wonder if the rod ought not first to have been used upon his father? It is a question (if we may modernize the instance) whether the old man at home was quite blameless in this matter. But so it is; men mistake enjoyment and the scope of pleasure; they forget that in the absence of discipline there can be no true profound enjoyment of any of the greatest gifts of God.

He who escapes discipline escapes one of the purest enjoyments; he who mistakes license for law goes downward to the pit at a rapid rate! Let us read: "And when he had spent all, there arose a mighty famine in that land; and he began to be in want" (v. 14).

The Cause of Famine

Such men help to bring about famines—men who eat all and produce nothing, men who are consumers and nonproducers. These are the men that make famines. A man that will eat up a whole wheatfield and do nothing in the way of sowing, is the man that will make a famine anywhere,—logically, necessarily. He is eating, appropriating, consuming, absorbing,—never working, never doing anything in return. Why, here is cause and effect. The man is eating the things that are round about him, and when the last meal is gone, he says, "There is a famine in the land." Of course there is. A man cannot always go on consuming and not producing without soon coming to the end of his patrimony, and finding a famine staring him in the face. "And when he had spent all" —all that he possessed admitted of being spent! You see my meaning? He has nothing that could not be spent. All that he had was outside of him. A man could get through the very stars of heaven if every one of them was a golden coin; a man could spend the sands upon the seashore if every sparkling atom was a silver coin! He could get through it all and be a pauper at the last!

Who is he, then, who cannot spend all? A man who lives spiritually, a man of character, of purpose, of high conception, of noble sympathy, a man who knows truth and loves truth never can spend his fortune. Once that fortune was attempted to be described, and the words of the description I remember well. "An inheritance incorruptible, undefiled, and that fadeth not away" (1 Peter 1:4). May I ask any young man what he possesses in the way of property, substance, security? If he says that all he has is outside of him, then I say it is very possible for him to get through it all, and at the last be compelled to face a famine. Gold can be spent; ideas cannot be wasted by the wise man. Some people scatter and yet increaseth; some withhold more than is meet, and it tendeth to poverty. Be sure of this, that any man in society who has not given back a fair equivalent for what he gets in the way of bread and dress and physical blessing, is the man who is working mischief in society—that man is one of the causes of destitution and famine.

A Sad Encounter With Poverty

"And he began to be in want" (v. 14).

A new experience came upon him. And oh! it is pitiful when a man who has never known want just begins to feel it. Better be born at the other end of things; better be born in poverty than in riches to be spent so. You should have seen him when he felt the first pang. It was pitiful! The man had a fine face; there was a gentle expression upon it at times, all the signs and tokens of refinement had not been quite taken out of it; and when the young man began to feel the pain of want, I was sorry of him. I saw his blanched face and saw him look round as if he might see his father somewhere, or his mother, and there was nothing but strangers, emptiness, desolation! He called out, and the mocking echo answered him. It was very sad, but it was right— it was right! If a man can take a course like that, and at the end of it be prosperous and joyful, having fullness of satisfaction; why, then, life is not worth having, and destiny is cruelty. I saw him in want, friendlessness, pain, hunger; and, though I feel that it might have been myself standing there, yet I own that it was right.

The Citizen and the Father

"And he went and joined himself to a citizen of the country; and he sent him into his fields to feed swine" (v. 15).

He was nothing to the citizen; the citizen cared nothing for him. The citizen did not say, "Let me see your hand, and I will tell you whether you were born a gentleman." He did not say, "How have you been brought up, young man? I will try to fall in, as far as possible, with the traditions of your youth." Nothing of the sort. No, no. It seems a little way from the man's father to the citizen—but oh, it is a long, long way! He left his father and went to the citizen. Both men! But the one was as a shining angel, and the other as a tormentor sent of providence to bring the young man to his senses. Yes, sir, you will say goodbye to your father and care nothing for him, but the first man you meet will be a rough one. Thank God for that! I thank God that there are rough men into whose hands young people fall, who have not known how to value a father's care and a mother's love. Young men must at some time or another come under the rod. They may delay the time of discipline, they may put off the time of judgment, but it comes upon them. Events are God's servants; the great purposes of heaven are working themselves out by events that we cannot number nor control. At the end it will be seen that there is a rod in the law, that there is a God on the throne, and that no man can do wrong without having judgment brought to bear upon him!

But could he do nothing better than feed swine? No! There was the great mischief. His father (again we modernize the instance) had never taught him a trade. Shame on his father! We blame the father more than we must blame the young man, in so far as this may be true. What could the young man do? Nothing. He had no skill in his fingers; he had no power of putting things together so as to make a living out of them. All he could do was the meanest of work—he could feed swine. Do you feel it to be somewhat a hardship, young man, that you are sent to work? It is the beginning of your prosperity, if rightly accepted. Do you say that you ought to have been something finer? There is time to prove how far you are worthy of elevation and honor. Meanwhile, whatever you are, do your work with all patience, believing that he who does so will in the end have a sufficient and appropriate reward. Let us follow

him in his menial employment and see how it fares
with him—with him who was once so pampered, who
was the delight of the household and the hope of his
father's life.

Bad Men Always Leave Dupes

"And he would fain have filled his belly with the husks
that the swine did eat; and no man gave unto him" (v.
16).

Is that true? It is literally true. Is it true in this
young man's experience? Then it is true in ours. We
cannot allow any dispute upon this for a moment, so
far as the book is concerned, because the same thing is
done every day among us. While the man spent his
substance in riotous living, he had friends and
companions; there were many who shared his bounty
and hospitality, but where are they now? They are not
within his call; they do not know him now. He spent
his money freely, and so long as he had any left they
lived with him, and were his friends. They prostituted
that sweet and holy name friend in order that they
might the better accomplish their own purposes. As
soon as they saw him lay down the last coin, and they
had helped him to devour it, they turned their backs
on him and declared they never knew him! No man
gave unto him, though he had given to so many men.

Bad men always disappoint their victims. Bad men
always make dupes and leave them. I would to God I
could teach that thoroughly and effectively. The bad
man cannot be a friend! The bad man who follows you,
tracks you about, waits for you at the warehouse door,
and spends your substance for you, cannot be a friend.
He looks like a friend, but he is an enemy in disguise.
"He apparently loves my company." Not a bit of it! He
loves what you have; he loves your money. "He seems
to prefer my society to anybody else's." He will ruin
you to suit his purpose! The bad man cannot be a
friend. He can be a sneak; a vampire; he can suck your
blood, but he cannot be a friend! Only he can be a
friend who can suffer for you, sympathize with you,

own you in darkness as well as in light, defend you in danger, as well as smile upon you in the time of prosperity.

I know this to be true. It has been burnt into our history as with a red-hot iron. This is no poet's fancy; this is no touch of dramatic genius—this is sadly, tragically, awfully true. It is not long since that a case in point occurred within the sphere of my own observation. A young man was taken up by a crafty villain, pursued by him, flattered by him—he could call upon this man to do what he pleased for him. There was plenty of money on the one side and a bottomless pit of perdition on the other, along with a smooth outside, a fair tongue, a gentle tone of expression. As long as there was any property to be squandered, the villain was at hand. He would do anything: set up houses for the young man and find him means of so-called enjoyment. He was his right-hand man, making all his arrangements, opening all the gates for him, and indicating the road that he was to take. And when the young man had spent thousands upon this policy, it came of course to a break, it came to a crisis. Where was his friend? Did he turn around and say, "I will be your friend still?" No. He said, "I will drag that young man through the mire."

This was not an accident—a single separate event standing by itself. It is a doctrine, a truth, that badness never can be sincere, that badness is always selfish, and that selfishness will always allure and destroy its dupes. And the young man's future went so. The old man at home perhaps had some difficulty in getting the property together. He used to be a workman himself, a man of good understanding and of great industry in matters of business, and it took him some 25 years to amass the property, and the young man spent it in a month! Be your own executor; you lay up money and you know not who will spend it. You say, "Five—seven—ten thousand for my youngest boy. That will be a nice start in life for him. He will never know hardship as I have known it. He will never have to eat brown bread as I have eaten it. He will begin in very comfortable circumstances and be able to take a very high position at once." Take care! He may spend it in a fortnight! At one toss of the dice your estate may be gone! He may be doing but a poor thing for his child who tries to turn nine thousand into ten thousand for him. Better send him to shoe-blacking, to crossing-sweeping, better make him a boy waiting in the shop, than so to train him as not to know the value of what you have amassed for his advantage. It may seem hard that he should begin where you began; but depend upon it that unless the young man be of singularly high principle and fine integrity, you are laying up for him that which will turn into a scorpion and sting him!

He Came to Himself

"And when he came to himself, he said, How many of my father's hired servants have bread enough and to spare, and I perish with hunger!" (v. 17).

Mark the beauty of this expression: "When he came to himself." All sin is insanity; all wickedness is madness. A wicked man is not himself. He has lost self-control, all his best memories have been darkened or forgotten, and he is no longer to be counted a sane man in the true and proper sense of that term. Wickedness blinds the intellectual faculties; disorders a man's vision—spiritual, intellectual, and moral; and gives him exaggerated notions of all other persons and things. A course of wickedness has a madhouse at the end of it!

How much we are mistaken upon this matter of insanity. We think only those persons insane who are imprisoned in asylums, who are restrained by a strait waistcoat, who have watchers and keepers appointed over them. We say about such, "Poor creatures, alas! They are insane!" But we don't realize that there is an insanity of wickedness, a moral insanity—and of all insanity moral insanity is the worst. Responsibility begins there. If a man's reason be blighted, then responsibility goes along with it. He cannot distinguish the right hand from the left in morals. But where the insanity is moral, where there is a love of evil, where iniquity is rolled under the tongue as a sweet morsel, then there is obligation, there is responsibility, and where there is responsibility there is the possibility of damnation!

"When he came to himself." He never would have come to himself if not for his poverty, his desertion, his pain. So Almighty God has strange ministers in his sanctuary. Not all his ministers are mere speakers of holy and beautiful words. He employs some grim teachers to instruct a certain class of mankind in the first principles of right: grief, hunger, pain, homelessness, ill-health, desertion. There are all the hired servants of the Father. He sends them out after sons that have left the old, dear home.

This young man had to thank his swine-feeding, his experience of famine, his homelessness, as the beginning of his better life. Many of us probably have had to do precisely the same thing. We found no religion in luxury; no altar in the carpeted room. As long as we had everything within reach and call, our hearts never went out of us in incense of praise, in utterance of prayer. Not until we were breadless, homeless, until we exchanged fatherhood for citizenship; not until we got under influences that were keenly bitter and tormenting in their effects, did we begin to know that we had done wrong. Some of us, again, have had to thank God for poverty, for ill-health, for friendlessness, for being left out on the streets without bread to eat or a pillow to rest upon while the rain dashed into our faces and no man knew us. It was then we called for God, and it was then the Father met us!

What did the young man say? Did he say, "Now I have taken this step, I cannot retrace it; I have said farewell to my father. I am not the man to succumb, to go back to my father's door and say, 'Please be kind enough to open this door to me again.' No, no; I will rise up from this state of poverty—I have been suffering by a heavy hand—I will yet make a man of myself; I will get back my fortune, I will renew my companions, and my latter time shall be better than my first"? If he had done so, he would have shown but another phase of his insanity.

He took the right course; he humbled himself; he got a right view of his way. He felt it to have been bad— bad in its purpose, bad in its conception, bad in its whole course. He said, "I will go without a defense; I will get up no argument; I will not explain how it came to be; I will just go and throw myself at his feet and say, 'Make a servant of me, only take me back again'." He won the battle then! The moment he threw off his pride, the moment he said, "I shall not stand before him, but fall down at his feet," he was victor! So long as there is a spark of pride left in a man, as between himself and God, a great battle has to be fought. So long as a man thinks he can make out a sufficient statement, an explanation of how he came to be wrong, and to do wrong, and can defend himself, in some degree at last—he is far from the kingdom of heaven.

Falling at Jesus Feet

What, then, is this that we have to say? Just this: There must be no excusings, no pleadings, no apologies, no arguments, no defenses. Man must surrender; he must say, "There is no health in me. I yield; I have grieved thee, insulted thee, wounded thee: it seems as if I never could be a son again. Make something of me in thy house still. I will keep a door, I will follow the poorest of thy servants to be his servant—only have me somewhere in thy care, dear, grieved, broken-hearted Father!" When a man begins to talk like that, he is saved—is saved!

The young man went forward with his speech, a beautiful speech, not a single strain of selfishness in it; all a speech of condemnation, self-renunciation. He got so far with it, and the father interrupted him, fell on his neck, and kissed him, and said, "Make a son of him again." It is God's way with the sinner. He never lets us finish our speech of penitence. We struggle and sob on to about a comma, or at most a semicolon, and then his great love comes down and says, "That will do; begin again; begin at the cross, my son; my child, begin at the cross!" Were I to talk through many hours, even until sunrise, I could say no more than this, that a right state of acceptance before God is a state of self-abhorrence, self-renunciation. So long as we stand, God will not have anything to do with us, because he cannot. But when we fall down at his feet; when we feel our nothingness and own it—it is then that he would put all heaven into our hearts.

NOTES

Bread Enough and to Spare

Charles Haddon Spurgeon (1834-1892) is undoubtedly the most famous minister of modern times. Converted in 1850, he united with the Baptists and very soon began to preach in various places. He became pastor of the Baptist church in Waterbeach in 1851, and three years later he was called to the decaying Park Street Church, London. Within a short time, the work began to prosper, a new church was built and dedicated in 1861, and Spurgeon became London's most popular preacher. In 1855, he began to publish his sermons weekly; and today they make up the fifty-seven volumes of *The Metropolitan Tabernacle Pulpit.* He founded a pastor's college and several orphanages.

This sermon is taken from *The Metropolitan Tabernacle Pulpit,* volume 17. It was the 1,000th sermon Spurgeon published. He preached it on Sunday morning, June 16, 1871.

7

BREAD ENOUGH AND TO SPARE

And when he came to himself, he said, How many of my
father's hired servants have bread enough and to spare,
and I perish with hunger! (Luke 15:17).

"HE CAME TO HIMSELF." The word may be applied to
one walking out of a deep swoon. He had been
unconscious of his true condition, and he had lost all
power to deliver himself from it. But now he was coming
round again, returning to consciousness and action.
The voice that shall awaken the dead aroused him; the
visions of his sinful trance all disappeared; his foul but
fascinating dreams were gone; he came to himself.

The word may also be applied to one recovering from
insanity. The prodigal son had played the madman, for
sin is madness of the worst kind. He had been
demented, he had traded bitter for sweet and sweet for
bitter, darkness for light and light for darkness. He
had injured himself, and he had done for his soul what
those possessed of devils in our Savior's time did for
their bodies when they wounded themselves with stones
and cut themselves with knives. The insane man does
not know himself to be insane, but as soon as he comes
to himself he painfully perceives the state from which
he is escaping. Returning then to true reason and sound
judgment, the prodigal came to himself.

Another illustration of the word may be found in the
old world fables of enchantment: when a man was
disenthralled from the magician's spell, he "came to
himself." Classic story has its legend of Circe, the
enchantress, who transformed men into swine. Surely
this young man in our parable had been degraded in
the same manner. He had lowered his manhood to the
level of the brutes. It should be the property of man to
have love to his kindred, to have respect for right, to

have some care for his own interest; this young man had lost all these proper attributes of humanity, and so had become as the beast that perishes. But as the poet sings of Ulysses, that he compelled the enchantress to restore his companions to their original form, so here we see the prodigal returning to manhood, looking away from his sensual pleasures, and commencing a course of conduct more consistent with his birth and parentage.

There are men here today perhaps who are still in this swoon. O God of heaven, arouse them! Some here who are morally insane. Lord, recover them! Divine Physician, put your cooling hand upon their fevered brow, and say to them, "I will; be thou made whole." Perhaps there are others here who have allowed their animal nature to reign supreme; may He who destroys the works of the devil deliver them from the power of Satan and give them power to become the sons of God. He shall have all the glory!

Aware of Two Thoughts

It appears that when the prodigal came to himself he was aware of two thoughts. Two facts were clean to him. There was plenty in his father's house, and he himself was famishing. May the two kindred spiritual facts have absolute power over all your hearts, if you are yet unsaved; for they were most certainly all-important and pressing truths. These are no fancies of one in a dream; no ravings of a maniac; no imaginations of one under fascination. It is most true that there is plenty of all good things in the Father's house, and that the sinner needs them. Nowhere else can grace be found or pardon gained. With God there is plenitude of mercy; let more venture to dispute this glorious truth. It is equally true that the sinner without God is perishing. He is perishing now; he will perish everlastingly. All that is worth having in his existence will be utterly destroyed, and he himself will only remain as a desolation. The owl and the bittern of misery and anguish will haunt the ruins of his nature forever and forever. If we could make unconverted men understand those two thoughts, what hopeful congregations we should have.

Alas! they forget that there is mercy only with God, and they fancy that it is to be found somewhere else. They try to slip away from the humbling fact of their own lost estate, and they imagine that perhaps there may be some back door of escape. They hope that, after all, they are not as bad as the Scripture declares, or that perchance it shall be right with them at the last, however wrong it may be with them now. Alas! my brethren, what shall we do with those who willfully shut their eyes to truths of which the evidence is overwhelming and the importance overpowering? I earnestly plead with those of you who know how to approach the throne of God in faith, to pray that he would now bring into captivity the unconverted heart and put these two strong fetters upon every unregenerate soul:

- There is abundant grace with God.
- There is utter destitution with themselves.

Bound with such fetter, and led into the presence of Jesus, the captive would soon receive the liberty of the children of God.

I intend to dwell this morning mainly upon the first thought, the master thought it seems to me, which was in the prodigal's mind—the thought that constrained him to say, "I will arise and go to my father." It was not, I think, the thought that he was perishing with hunger that brought him home, but the impulse toward his father found its mainspring in the consideration, "How many of my father's hired servants have bread enough and to spare!" (v. 17). The plenty, the abundance, the superabundance of the father's house, was what attracted him to return home. Likewise many, many a soul has been led to seek God when it has fully believed that there was abundant mercy for him. My desire this morning shall be to put plainly before every sinner here the exceeding abundance of the grace of

God in Christ Jesus, hoping that the Lord will find out those who are his sons, and that they may catch at these words, and as they hear of the abundance of the bread in the Father's house, may say, "I will arise and go to my Father."

Consider the Father

Let us consider for a short time *the more than abundance of all good things in the Father's house.* What do you need this morning, awakened sinner? Of all that you need, there is with God an all-sufficient, a superabounding supply; "bread enough and to spare." Let us prove this to you.

First, consider the Father himself. Whoever will rightly consider the Father will at once perceive that there can be no stint to mercy, no bound to the possibilities of grace. What is the nature and character of the Supreme? "Is He harsh or loving?" asks one. The Scripture answers the question, not by telling us that God is loving, but by assuring us that God is love. God Himself is love; it is His very essence. It is not that love is in God, but that God Himself is love. Can there be a more concise and more positive way of saying that the love of God is infinite?

You cannot measure God himself; your conceptions cannot grasp the grandeur of His attributes, neither can you tell the dimensions of His love, nor conceive the fulness of it. Only know this, that as high as the heavens are above the earth, so are His ways higher than your ways, and his thoughts higher than your thoughts. His mercy endures forever. He pardons iniquity, and passes by the transgression of the remnant of His heritage. He retains not his anger forever, because he delights in mercy. "Thou, Lord, art good, and ready to forgive, and plenteous in mercy unto all them that call upon thee" (Ps. 86:5). "Thy mercy is great above the heavens" (Ps. 57:10). "The Lord is very pitiful, and of tender mercy" (Jas. 5:11).

If divine love alone should not seem sufficient for your salvation, remember that with the Father to whom the sinner returns, there is as much of wisdom as there is of grace. Is your case a very difficult one? He that made you can heal you. Are your diseases strange and complex? He that fashioned the ear, can He not remove its deafness? He that made the eye, can He not enlighten it if it be blind? No mischief can have happened to you, but what He who is your God can recover you from it. Matchless wisdom cannot fail to meet the intricacies of your case.

Neither can there be any failure of power with the Father. Do you not know that He who made the earth, and stretched out the heavens like a tent to dwell in, has no bound to His strength, nor limit to His might? If you need omnipotence to lift you up from the slough into which you have fallen, omnipotence is ready to deliver you, if you cry to the strong for strength. Though you should need all the force with which the Creator made the worlds, and all the strength with which He bears up the pillars of the universe, all that strength and force should be laid out for your good, if you would in faith seek mercy at the hand of God in Christ Jesus. None of His power shall be against you, none of His wisdom shall plan your overthrow; but love shall reign in all, and every attribute of God will become subservient to your salvation.

Oh, when I think of sin I cannot understand how a sinner can be saved; but when I think of God, and look into His heart, I understand how readily He can forgive. "Look into His heart," says one. "How can we do that?" Has He not laid bare His heart to you? Do you inquire where He has done this? I answer, yonder, upon Calvary's cross. What was in the very center of the divine heart? What, but the person of the Well-beloved, His only begotten Son? And He hath taken His only begotten and nailed Him to the cross, because, if I may venture so to speak, He loved sinners better than His Son. He spared not His Son, but He spares the sinner. He poured out His wrath upon His Son and made Him the substitute for sinners, that He might lavish love upon the guilty who deserved His anger. O soul, if you are lost, it is not from any want of grace or wisdom or power in the Father; if you perish, it is not because God is hard to move or unable to save. If you become a castaway, it is not because the Eternal refused to hear your cries for pardon or rejected your faith in Him. On your own head be your blood, if your soul be lost. If you starve, you starve because you choose to starve. In the Father's house there is "bread enough and to spare."

Consider the Son

But, now, consider a second matter which may set this more clearly before us. Think of the Son of God, who is indeed the true bread of life for sinners. Sinner, I return to my personal address. You need a Savior; and you may well be encouraged when you see that a Savior is provided—provided by God, since it is certain he would not make a mistake in the provision.

But consider who the Savior is. He is himself God. Jesus who came from heaven for our redemption was not an angel, else might we tremble to trust the weight of our sin upon Him. He was not mere man, or He could but have suffered as a substitute for one, if indeed for one; but He was very God of very God, in the beginning with the Father. And does such a one come to redeem? Is there room to doubt as to His ability, if that be the fact? I do confess this day, that if my sins were ten thousand times heavier then they are, yea, and if I had all the sins of his crowd in addition piled upon me, I could trust Jesus with them all at this moment now that I know Him to be the Christ of God. He is the mighty God, and by His pierced hand the burden of our sins is easily removed. He blotteth out our sins and casts them into the depths of the sea.

But think of what Jesus the Son of God has done. He who was God, and thus blessed forever, left the throne and royalties of heaven, and stooped to yonder manger. There He lies; His mother wraps Him in swaddling clothes, He hangs upon her breast. The Infinite is clothed as an infant, the Invisible is made manifest in flesh, the Almighty is linked with weakness, for our sakes. Oh, matchless stoop of condescension! If the Redeemer God does this in order to save us, shall it be thought a thing impossible for Him to save the vilest of the vile? Can anything be too hard for Him who comes from heaven to earth to redeem?

Pause not because of astonishment, but press onward. Do you see Him who was God over all, blessed forever, living more than 30 years in the midst of the sons of men, bearing the infirmities of manhood, taking upon Himself our sickness, and sharing our sorrows? His feet grew weary with treading the acres of Palestine; His body often became faint with hunger and thirst and labor; His knees were knit to the earth with midnight prayer; His eyes grew red with weeping (for ofttimes Jesus wept); He was tempted in all points like as we are.

Matchless spectacle! An incarnate God dwells among sinners and endures their contradiction! What glory flashed forth ever and anon from the midst of His lowliness! It is a glory that would render faith in Him inevitable. Thou who didst walk the sea: Thou who didst raise the dead, it is not rational to doubt Thy power to forgive sins! Didst Thou not thyself put it so when Thou badest the man take up his bed and walk? Which is easier to say, "Thy sins be forgiven thee;" or to say, "Rise up and walk?" Assuredly He is able to save to the uttermost them that come unto God by Him: He was able even here on earth in weakness to forgive sins, much more now that He is seated in His glory. He is exalted on high to be a Prince and a Savior, to give repentance and remission of sins.

But, ah! the master proof that in Christ Jesus there is "bread enough and to spare," is the cross. Will you follow me a moment, will you follow Him, rather, to Gethsemane? Can you see the bloody sweat as it falls upon the ground in His agony? Can you think of His scourging before Herod and Pilate? Can you trace Him along the *Via Dolorosa* of Jerusalem? Will your tender hearts endure to see Him nailed to the tree, and lifted up to bleed and die? This is but the shell; as for the inward kernel of His sufferings no language can describe it, neither can conception peer into it. The everlasting God laid sin on Christ, and where the sin was laid there fell the wrath. "It pleased the Lord to bruise Him; He hath put him to grief" (Isa. 53:10).

Now He that died upon the cross was God's only begotten Son. Can you conceive a limit to the merit of such a Savior's death? I know there are some who think it necessary to their system of theology to limit the merit of the blood of Jesus. If my system of theology needed such a limitation, I would cast it to the winds. I cannot, dare not, allow the thought to find a lodging in my mind; it seems so near akin to blasphemy. In Christ's finished work I see an ocean of merit; my plummet finds no bottom, my eye discovers no shore. There must be sufficient efficacy in the blood of Christ, if God had so willed it, to have saved not only all this world, but ten thousand worlds, had they transgressed the Maker's law. Once you admit infinity into the matter, limit is out of the question. Having a divine person for an offering, it is not consistent to conceive of limited value; bound and measure are terms inapplicable to the divine sacrifice. The intent of the divine purpose fixes the application of the infinite offering, but does not change it into a finite work. In the atonement of Christ Jesus there is "bread enough and to spare;" even as Paul wrote to Timothy, "He is the Savior of all men, specially of those that believe" (1 Tim. 4:10).

Consider the Spirit

But now let me lead you to another point of solemnly joyful consideration, and that is the Holy Spirit. To believe and love the Trinity is to possess the key of theology. We spoke of the Father, we spoke of the Son; let us now speak of the Holy Spirit. We do Him all too little honor, for the Holy Spirit condescends to come to earth and dwell in our hearts. Notwithstanding all our provocations, He still abides within His people. Now, sinner, you need a new life and you need holiness, for both of these are necessary to make you fit for heaven. Is there a provision for this? The Holy Spirit is provided and given in the covenant of grace; and surely in Him there is "enough and to spare." What cannot the Holy Spirit do? Being divine, nothing can be beyond His power. Look at what He has already done.

He moved upon the face of chaos, and brought it into order; all the beauty of creation arose beneath His molding breath. We ourselves must confess with Elihu, "The Spirit of God, hath made me, and the breath of the Almighty hath given me life" (Job 33:4).

Think of the great deeds of the Holy Spirit at Pentecost, when unlearned men spoke with tongues of which they knew not a syllable, and the flames of fire upon them were also within them, so that their hearts burned with zeal and courage to which they hitherto had been strangers.

Think of the Holy Spirit's work on such a one as Saul of Tarsus. That persecutor foams blood, he is a very wolf, he would devour the saints of God at Damascus, and yet, within a few moments, you hear him say, "Who art thou, Lord?" (Acts 9:5) and yet again, "Lord, what wilt thou have me to do?" (v. 6). His heart is changed; the Spirit of God has created it anew; the adamant is melted in a moment into wax.

Many of us stand before you as the living monuments of what the Holy Spirit can do, and we can assure you from our own experience, that there is no inward evil that He cannot overcome, no lustful desire of the flesh that He cannot subdue, no hardness of the affections that He cannot melt. Is anything too hard for the Lord? Is the Spirit of the Lord straitened? Surely no sinner can be beyond the possibilities of mercy when the Holy Spirit condescends to be the agent of human conversion. O sinner, if you perish, it is not because the Holy Spirit lacks power, or the blood of Jesus lacks efficacy, or the Father fails in love; it is because you believe not in Christ, but abide in willful rebellion, refusing the abundant bread of life placed before you.

Consider God's Great Message

And now a few rapid sentences upon other things, which will show still further the greatness of the provision of divine mercy. Observe well that *throughout all the ages God has been sending one prophet after another,* and these prophets have been succeeded by apostles, and these by martyrs and confessors, and pastors and evangelists, and teachers. All these have been commissioned by the Lord in regular succession. What has been the message they have had to deliver? They have all pointed to Christ, the great deliverer. Moses and the prophets all spoke of Him, and so have all truly God-sent ambassadors.

Do you think, sinner, that God has made all this fuss about a trifle? Has He sent all these servants to call you to a table insufficiently furnished? Has He multiplied his invitations through so long a time to bid you and others come to a provision which is not, after all, sufficient for them? Oh, it cannot be! God is not mocked, neither does he mock poor needy souls. The stores of his mercy are sufficient for the utmost emergencies.

> Rivers of love and mercy here
> In a rich ocean join;
> Salvation in abundance flows,
> Like floods of milk and wine.
>
> Great God, the treasures of thy love
> Are everlasting mines,
> Deep as our helpless miseries are,
> And boundless as our sins.

Recollect again, that *God has been pleased to stake his honor upon the gospel.* Men desire a name, and God also is jealous of His glory. Now, what has God been pleased to select for His name? Is it not the conversion and salvation of men? When instead of the brier shall come up the myrtle tree, and instead of the thorn shall come up the fir tree, it shall be to the Lord for a name, for an everlasting sign that shall not be cut off. And do you think God will get a name by saving little sinners by a little Savior? Ah! His great name comes from washing out stains as black as hell, and pardoning sinners who were foulest of the foul. Is there one monstrous rebel here who is qualified to glorify God greatly, because his salvation will be the wonder of angels and the amazement of devils? I hope there is.

O thou most degraded, black, loathsome sinner, nearest to being a damned sinner, if this voice can reach you, I challenge you to come and prove whether God's mercy is not a match for your sin. Thou Goliath sinner, come hither; you will find that God can slay your enmity and make you yet his friend and his loving and adoring servant, because great forgiveness shall secure great love. Such is the greatness of divine mercy, that "where sin abounded, grace doth much more abound" (Rom. 5:20).

Do you think, again, O sinner, that Jesus Christ came out of heaven to do a little deed, and to provide a slender store of mercy? Do you think He went up to Calvary and down to the grave, and all, that He might do a commonplace thing, and provide a stinted, narrow, limited salvation, such as unbelief would imagine His redemption to be? No. We speak of the labors of Hercules, but these were child's play compared with the labors of Christ who slew the lion of hell, turned a purifying stream through the Augean stables of man's sin, and cleansed them, and performed ten thousand miracles besides. And will you so depreciate Christ as to imagine that what He has accomplished is after all, little, so little that it is not enough to save you?

If it were in my power to single out the man who has been the most dishonest, most licentious, most drunken, most profane—in three words, most earthly, sensual, devilish—I would repeat the challenge I gave just now, and bid them draw near to Jesus, and see whether the fountain filled with Christ's atoning blood cannot wash him white. I challenge him at this instant to come and cast himself at the dear Redeemer's feet, and see if he will say, "I cannot save thee, thou hast sinned beyond my power." It shall never, never, never be, for He is able to the uttermost to save. He is a Savior, and a great one. Christ will be honored by the grandeur of the grace He bestows upon the greatest of offenders. There is in Him pardon "enough and to spare."

I must leave this point, but I cannot do so without adding that I think "BREAD ENOUGH AND TO SPARE" might be taken for the motto of the gospel. I believe in particular redemption, and that Christ laid down his life for his sheep; but, as I have already said, I do not believe in the limited value of that redemption. How else could I dare to read the words of John, "He is the propitiation for our sins: and not for ours only, but also for the sins of the whole world" (1 John 2:2). There is a sure portion for His own elect, but there is also over and above "to spare." I believe in the electing love that will save all its objects—"bread enough;" but I believe in boundless benevolence, "Bread enough *and to spare.*"

We, when we have a purpose to accomplish, put forth the requisite quantity of strength and no more, for we must be economical, we must not waste our limited store. Even charity gives the poor man no more than he absolutely needs. But when God feeds the multitude, He spreads the board with imperial bounty. Our water-cart runs up and down the favored road, but when heaven's clouds would favor the good man's field, they deluge whole nations, and even pour themselves upon the sea. There is no real waste with God; but at the same time there is no stint. "BREAD ENOUGH AND TO SPARE." Write that inscription over the house of mercy, and let every hungry passerby be encouraged by it to enter in and eat.

Enough for the Servants

We must now pass on to a second consideration, and dwell very briefly on it. According to the text, there was not only bread enough in the house, but *the lowest in the Father's house enjoyed enough and to spare.*

We can never make a parable run on all fours, therefore we cannot find the exact counterpart of the "hired servants." I understand the prodigal to have meant this, that the very lowest menial servant employed by his father had bread to eat, and had "bread enough to spare." Now, how should we translate this? Why, sinner, the very lowest creature that God has made, that has not sinned against Him, is well supplied and has abounding happiness. There are adaptations for pleasure in the organizations of the lowest animals. See how the gnats dance in the summer's sunbeam; hear the swallows as they scream with delight when on the wing. He who cares for birds and insects will surely care for men. God who hears the ravens when they cry, will He not hear the returning penitent? He gives these insects happiness; did He mean me to be wretched? Surely He who opens His hand and supplies the lack of every living thing, will not refuse to open His hand and supply my needs if I seek His face.

Yet I must not make these lowest creatures to be the hired servants. Whom shall I then select among men? I will put it thus. The very worst of sinners that have come to Christ have found grace "enough and to spare," and the very least of saints who dwell in the house of the Lord find love "enough and to spare." Take then the most guilty of sinners, and see how bountifully the Lord treats them when they turn unto Him. Did not some of you, who are yourselves unconverted, once know persons who were at least as bad, perhaps more outwardly immoral than yourselves? Well, they have been converted, though you have not been; and when they were converted, what was their testimony? Did the blood of Christ avail to cleanse them? Oh, yes; and more than cleanse them, for it added to beauty not their own. They were naked once; was Jesus able to clothe them? Was there a sufficient covering in His righteousness? Ah, yes! and adornment was superadded; they received not a bare apparel, but a royal raiment.

You have seen others thus liberally treated, does not this induce you also to come? Some of us need not confine our remarks to others, for we can speak personally of ourselves. We came to Jesus as full of sin as ever *you* can be, and felt ourselves beyond measure lost and ruined; but, oh, His tender love! I could sooner stand here and weep than speak to you of it. My soul melts in gratitude when I think of the infinite mercy of God to me in the honor when I came seeking mercy at His hands. Oh! why will not you also come? May His Holy Spirit sweetly draw you! I proved that there was bread enough, mercy enough, forgiveness enough, and to spare. Come along, come along, poor guilty one. Come along! There is room enough for you.

Now, if the chief of sinners bear this witness, so do *the most obscure of saints.* If we could call forth from his seat a weak believer in God, who is almost unknown in the church, one who sometimes questions whether he is indeed a child of God, and would be willing to be a hired servant so long as he might belong to God, and if I were to ask him, "Now after all, how has the Lord dealt with you?" what would be his reply?

You have many afflictions, doubts and fears, but have you any complaints against your Lord? When you have waited upon Him for daily grace, has He denied you? When you have been full of troubles, has He refused you comfort? When you have been plunged in distress, has He declined to deliver you? The Lord himself asks, "Have I been a wilderness unto Israel?" Testify against the Lord, you His people, if you have anything against Him. Hear, O heavens, and give ear, O earth, whosoever there be in God's service who has found Him a hard taskmaster, let him speak. Among the angels before Jehovah's throne, and among men redeemed on earth, if there be anyone who can say he has been dealt with unjustly or treated with ungenerous churlishness, let him lift up his voice! But there is not one.

Even the devil himself, when he spoke of God and of His servant Job, said, "Doth Job fear God for nought?" (Job 1:9). Of course he did not: God will not let His servants serve Him for nought; He will pay them superabundant wages, and they shall all bear witness that at His table there is "bread enough and to spare." Now, if these still enjoy the bread of the Father's house, these who were once great sinners, these who are now only very commonplace saints, surely, sinners, it should encourage you to say, "I will arise and go to my Father," for his hired servants "have bread enough and to spare."

Enough for the Multitudes

Notice in the third place that the text dwells upon *the multitude of those who have "bread enough and to spare."* The prodigal lays an emphasis upon that word, *"How many* hired servants of my father's!" He was thinking of their great number, and counting them over. He thought of those who tended the cattle, of those who went out with the camels, of those who watched the sheep, and those who minded the corn, and those who waited in the house. He ran them over in his mind. His father was great in the land and had many servants, yet he knew that they all had of the best food "enough and to spare." "Why should I perish with hunger? I am only one. Although my hunger seem insatiable, it is but one belly that has to be filled, and, lo, my father fills hundreds, thousands every day. Why should I perish with hunger?"

Now, O you awakened sinner, you who feels this morning your sin and misery, think of the numbers upon whom God has bestowed His grace already. Think of the countless hosts in heaven. If you were introduced there today, you would find it as easy to tell the stars, or the sands of the sea, as to count the multitudes that are before the throne even now.

They have come from the east and from the west, and they are sitting down with Abraham, with Isaac, and with Jacob, and there is room enough for you. And beside those in heaven, think of those on earth. Blessed be God, His elect on earth are to be counted by millions, I believe, and the days are coming, brighter days than these, when there shall be multitudes upon multitudes brought to know the Savior, and to rejoice in Him. The Father's love is not for a few only, but for an exceeding great company. A number that no man can number will be found in heaven. Now, a man can number a very great amount. Set to work your Newtons, your calculators. They can count great numbers, but God and God alone can tell the multitude of His redeemed.

Now, sinner, you are but one great sinner as you are and the mercy of God that embraces millions must have room enough in it for you. The sea that holds the whales and creeping things innumerable, do you say, "It will overflow its banks if I bathe therein"? Of the sun that floods the universe with light, canst you say, "I should exhaust his beams if I should ask him to enlighten my darkness"? Say not so. If you came to yourself you will not tolerate such a thought, but you will remember with hope the richness of the Father's grace, even though your own poverty stare you in the face.

Hanging by a Thread

Let us add a few words to close with, close grappling words to some of you to whom God has sent His message this morning, and whom He intends to save. O, you who have been long hearers of the gospel, and who know it well in theory, but have felt none of the power of it in your hearts, let me now remind you where and what you are! You are perishing. As the Lord liveth, there is but a step between you and death. Only a step, nay, only a breath between you and hell. Sinner, if at this moment your heart should cease its beating, and there are a thousand causes that might produce that result before the clock ticks again, you would be in the flames of divine wrath. Can you bear to be in such peril? If you were hanging over a rock by a slender thread that must soon break, and if you would then fall headlong down a terrible precipice, you would not sleep, but be full of alarm. May you have sense enough, wit enough, grace enough, to be alarmed until you escape from the wrath to come.

Recollect, however, that while you are perishing, you are perishing in sight of plenty. You are famishing where a table is abundantly spread. What is more, there are those whom you know now sitting at that table and feasting. What sad perversity for a man to persist in being starved in the midst of a banquet, where others are being satisfied with good things!

But I think I hear you say, "I fear I have no right to come to Jesus." I will ask you this: Have you any right to say that till you have been denied? Did you ever try to go to Christ? Has He ever rejected you? If then you have never received a repulse, why do you wickedly imagine that He would repel you? Wickedly, I say, for it is an offense against the Christ who opened His heart upon the cross, to imagine that He could repel a penitent.

Have you any right to say, "But I am not one of those for whom mercy is provided"? Who told you so? Have you climbed to heaven and read the secret records of God's election? Has the Lord revealed a strange decree to you, and said, "Go and despair, I will have no pity on you"? If you say that God has so spoken, I do not believe you. In this sacred book is recorded what God has said. Here is the sure word of testimony, and in it I find it said of no humble seeker that God hath shut him out from His grace. What gives you a right to invent such a fiction in order to secure your own damnation? Instead, there is much in the Word of God and elsewhere to encourage you to come to Christ. He has not repelled one sinner yet; that is good to begin with. And it is not likely that He would, for since He died to save sinners, why should He reject them when they seek to be saved?

You say, "I am afraid to come to Christ." Is that wise? I have heard of a poor navigator who had been converted, who had but little education, but who knew the grace of our Lord Jesus Christ, and when dying, very cheerfully and joyfully longed to depart. His wife said to him, "But, mon, ain't ye afeared to stand before the judge?" "Woman," said he, "why should I be afeared of a man as died for me?" Oh, why should you be afraid of Christ who died for sinners? The idea of being afraid of Him should be banished by the fact that He shed his blood for the guilty. You have much reason to believe from the very fact that He died, that He will receive you. Besides, you have His word for it, for He said, "Him that cometh to me I will in no wise cast out"—for no reason, and in no way, and on no occasion, and under no pretence, and for no motive. "I will not cast him out," says the original. "Him that cometh to me I will in no wise cast out" (John 6:37). You say it is too good to be true that there can be pardon for you. This is a foolish measuring of God's corn with your bushel, and because it seems too good a thing for you to receive, you fancy it is too good for God to bestow. Let the greatness of the good news be one reason for believing that the news is true, for it is so like God.

> Who is a pardoning God like thee?
> Or who hath grace so rich and free?

Because the gospel assures us that He forgives great sins through a great Savior, it looks as if it were true, since He is so great a God.

There Is Hope

What should be the result of all this with every sinner here at this time? I think this good news should arouse those who have almost gone to sleep through despair. The sailors have been pumping the vessel, the leaks are gaining, she is going down, the captain is persuaded she must be a wreck. Depressed by such evil tidings, the men refuse to work; and since the boats are all broken in and they cannot make a raft, they sit down in despair. Presently the captain has better news for them. "She will float," he says. "The wind is abating too, the pumps tell upon the water, the leak can be reached yet." See how they work; with what cheery courage they toil on, because there is hope! Soul, there is hope! *There is hope!* THERE IS HOPE! To the harlot, to the thief, to the drunkard.

"There is no hope," says Satan. Liar that you are, get back to your den; for you there is no hope. But for fallen man, though he be in the mire of sin up to his very neck, though he be at the gates of death, while he lives there is hope. There is hope for hopeless souls in the Savior.

In addition to arousing us, this hope ought to elevate the sinner's thoughts. Some years ago, there was a crossing-sweeper in Dublin. He stood at the corner with his broom, and in all probability his highest thoughts were to keep the crossing clean and look for the pence. One day, a lawyer put his hand on his shoulder and said to him, "My good fellow, do you know that you are heir to a fortune of ten thousand pounds a year?" "Do you mean it?" said he. "I do," he said. "I have just received the information. I am sure you are the man." He walked away, *and he forgot his broom.* Are you astonished? Why, who would not have forgotten a broom when suddenly made possessor of ten thousand a year? So, I pray that some poor sinners, who have been thinking of the pleasures of the world, when they hear that there is hope, and that there is heaven to be had, will forget the deceitful pleasures of sin, and follow after higher and better things.

Should this hope not also purify the mind? The prodigal, when he said, "I will arise and go to my father," became in a measure reformed from that very moment. How, say you? Why, he left the swine-trough. What's more, he left the wine cup, and he left the harlots. He did not go with the harlots on his arm and with the wine cup in his hand, and say, "I will take these with me, and go to my father." It could not be. These were all left, and though he had no goodness to bring, yet he did not try to keep his sins and come to Christ.

A Final Warning

I shall close with this remark, because it will act as a sort of *caveat,* and be a fit word to season the wide invitations of the free gospel. Some of you, I fear, will make mischief even out of the gospel. You will dare to take the cross and use it for a gibbet for your souls. If God is so merciful, you will go therefore and sin the more; and because grace is freely given, therefore you will continue in sin that grace may abound. If you do this, I would solemnly remind you I have no grace to preach to such as you. "Your damnation is just;" it is the word of inspiration, and the only one I know that is applicable to such as you are. But every needy, guilty soul that desires a Savior is told today to believe in Jesus, that is, trust in the substitution and sacrifice of Christ, trust Him to take your sin and blot it out; trust Him to take your soul and save it. Trust Christ entirely, and you are forgiven this very moment. You are saved this very instant, and you may rejoice now in the fact that being justified by faith you have peace with God through Jesus Christ our Lord. O come ye, come ye; come and welcome; come ye now to the Redeemer's blood.

Holy Spirit, compel them to come in, that the house of mercy may be filled. Amen, and Amen.

NOTES

The Prodigal and His Brother

Frederick W. Robertson (1816-1853) wanted to be a soldier, but he yielded to his father's decision that he take orders in the Anglican church. The courage that he would have shown on the battlefield, he displayed in the pulpit, where he fearlessly declared truth as he saw it. Never strong physically, he experienced deep depression; he questioned his faith, and he often wondered if his ministry was doing any good. He died a young man, in great pain, but in great faith and courage. He had ministered for only 6 years at Trinity Chapel, Brighton, but today his printed sermons have taken his brave message around the world.

This one is from his *Sermons, Third Series,* published in 1900 in London by Kegan Paul, Trench, Trubner and Company. Robertson preached it on February 21, 1853.

Frederick W. Robertson

8

THE PRODIGAL AND HIS BROTHER

And he said unto him, Son, thou are ever with me, and all that I have is thine. It was fitting that we should make merry, and be glad; for this, thy brother, was dead, and is alive again; and was lost, and is found (Luke 15:31, 32).

THERE ARE TWO classes of sins. There are some sins by which man crushes, wounds, and malevolently injures his brother man: those sins which speak of a bad, tyrannical, and selfish heart. Christ met those with denunciation. There are other sins by which a man injures himself. There is a life of reckless indulgence. There is a career of yielding to ungovernable propensities, which most surely conducts to wretchedness and ruin, but makes a man an object of compassion rather than of condemnation.

The reception that sinners of this class met from Christ was marked by strange and pitying mercy. There was no maudlin sentiment on his lips. He called sin sin, and guilt guilt. Yet there were sins that His lips scourged, and others over which, containing in themselves their own scourge, His heart bled. That which was melancholy, and marred, and miserable in this world was more congenial to the heart of Christ than that which was proudly happy. It was in the midst of a triumph, and all the pride of a procession, that He paused to weep over ruined Jerusalem.

If we ask why the character of Christ was marked by this melancholy condescension, it is that He was in the midst of a world of ruins, and there was nothing here to gladden, but very much to touch with grief. He was here to restore that which was broken down and crumbling into decay. An enthusiastic antiquarian, standing amid the fragments of an ancient temple surrounded by dust and moss, broken pillar, and defaced architrave, with magnificent projects in his mind of restoring all this to *former* majesty, to draw out to light from mere rubbish the ruined glories, and therefore stooping down amongst the dank ivy and the rank nettles; such was Christ amidst the wreck of human nature. He was striving to lift it out of its degradation. He was searching out in revolting places that which had fallen down, that He might build it up again in fair proportions a holy temple to the Lord.

Therefore He labored among the guilty. Therefore He was with the companion of outcasts. Therefore He spoke tenderly and lovingly to those whom society counted undone. Therefore He loves to bind up the bruised and the brokenhearted. Therefore His breath fanned the spark that seemed dying out in the wick of the expiring taper, when men thought that it was too late, and that the hour of *hopeless* profligacy was come. It was that feature in His character, that tender, hoping, encouraging spirit of His which the prophet Isaiah fixed upon as characteristic. "A bruised reed shall He not break" (Isa. 42:3).

It was an illustration of this spirit which He gave in the parable that forms the subject of our consideration today. We find the occasion which drew it from Him in the commencement of this chapter, "Then drew near unto Him all the publicans and sinners for to hear Him. And the Pharisees and scribes murmured, saying, This man receiveth sinners, and eateth with them" (vv. 1, 2). It was then that Christ condescended to offer an excuse or an explanation of His conduct. And His excuse was this: It is natural, humanly natural, to rejoice more over that which has been recovered than over that which has never been lost. He proved that by three illustrations taken from human life. The first illustration intended to show the feelings of Christ in winning back a sinner. It showed the joy the shepherd feels in the recovery of a sheep from the mountain wilderness. The second was the satisfaction a person feels for a recovered coin. The last one was the gladness that attends the restoration of an erring son.

Now the three parables are alike in this. They all describe more or less vividly the feelings of the Redeemer on the recovery of the lost. But the third parable differs from the other two in this. Besides the feelings of the Savior, it gives us a multitude of particulars about the feelings, and steps, and the motives of the penitent who is reclaimed to goodness. In the first two the thing lost is a coin or a sheep. It would not be possible to find any picture of remorse or gladness there. But in the third parable the thing lost is not a lifeless thing, nor a mute thing, but a being, the workings of whose human heart are all described. So the subject opened out to us is a more extensive one—not merely the feelings of the finder, God in Christ, but besides that, the sensations of the wanderer himself.

In dealing with this parable, here is the approach we will adopt. We will look at the picture it draws of— 1). God's treatment of the penitent, and 2). God's expostulation with the saint. God's treatment of the penitent divides itself in this parable into three distinct epochs. The period of alienation, the period of repentance, and the circumstances of a penitent reception. We shall consider all these in turn.

The Alienation of Man's Heart

The first truth exhibited in this parable is the alienation of man's heart from God. Homelessness, distance from our Father—that is man's state by nature in this world. The youngest son gathered everything together and took his journey into a *far* country. Brethren, this is the history of worldliness. It is a state far from God; in other words, it is a state of homelessness. And now let us ask what that means. To English hearts it is not necessary to expound elaborately the infinite meanings which cluster round that blessed expression "home." Home is the one place in all this world where hearts are sure of each other. It is the place of confidence. It is the place where we tear off that mask of guarded and suspicious coldness which the world forces us to wear in self-defense and where we pour out the unreserved communications of full and confiding hearts. It is the spot where expressions of tenderness gush out without any sensations of awkwardness and without any dread of ridicule. Let a man travel where he will, home is the place to which "his heart untraveled fondly turns." He is to double all pleasure there. He is there to divide all pain. A *happy home* is the single spot of rest which a man has upon this earth for the cultivation of his noblest sensibilities.

And now my brethren, if that be the description of home, is God's place of rest your home? Walk abroad and alone by night. That awful other world in the stillness and the solemn deep of the eternities above, is it your home? Those graves that lie beneath you, holding in them the infinite secret, and stamping upon all earthly loveliness the mark of frailty and change and fleetingness—are those graves the prospect to which in bright days and dark days you can turn without dismay? God in His splendors—dare we feel with Him affectionate and familiar, so that trial comes softened by this feeling—it is my Father, and enjoyment can be taken with a frank feeling; my Father has given it to me, without grudging, to make me happy? All that is wrapped up in having a home in God.

Are we at home there? Why there is demonstration in our very childhood that we are not at home with that other world of God's. An infant fears to be alone, because he feels he is not alone. He trembles in the dark, because he is conscious of the presence of the world of spirits. Long before he has been told tales of terror, there is an instinctive dread of the supernatural in the infant mind. It is the instinct which we have from childhood that gives us the feeling of another world. And mark, brethren, if the child is not at home in the thought of that world of God's, the deep of darkness and eternity is around him—God's home, but not his home, for his flesh creeps. And that feeling grows through life; not the fear—when the child becomes a man he gets over fear—but the dislike. The man feels as much aversion as the child for the world of spirits.

Sunday comes. It breaks across the current of his worldliness. It suggests thoughts of death and judgment and everlasting existence. Is that home? Can the worldly man feel Sunday life a foretaste of his Father's mansion? If we could but know how many have come here today, not to have their souls lifted up heavenwards, but from curiosity, or idleness, or criticism, it would give us an appalling estimate of the number who are living in a far country "having no hope, and without God in the world" (Eph. 2:12).

The Unsatisfying Nature of Worldly Happiness

The second truth conveyed to us in this parable is the unsatisfying nature of worldly happiness. The outcast son tried to satiate his appetite with husks. A husk is an empty thing; it is a thing that looks extremely like food, and promises as much as food; but it is not food. It is a thing which when chewed will calm the appetite, but leaves the emaciated body without nourishment. Earthly happiness is a husk. We do not say that there is no satisfaction in the pleasures of a worldly life. That would be an overstatement of the truth. There is something in it, or else why would men persist in living for it? The cravings of man's appetite may be slowed by things that cannot satisfy him.

Every new pursuit contains in it a new hope; and it is long before hope is bankrupt. But my brethren, it is strange if a man has not found out long before he has reached the age of 30, that everything here is empty and disappointing. The nobler his heart and the more unquenchable his hunger for the high and the good, the sooner will he find that out. Bubble after bubble bursts, each bubble tinted with the celestial colors of the rainbow, and each leaving in the hand which crushes it a cold, damp drop of disappointment. All that is described in Scripture by the emphatic metaphor of "sowing the wind and reaping the whirlwind" (Hosea 8:7), the whirlwind of blighted hopes and unreturned feelings and crushed expectations—that is the harvest the world gives you to reap.

But why is this world unsatisfying? Brethren, it is the grandeur of the soul God has given us, which makes it insatiable in its desires—with an infinite void that cannot be filled up. A soul that was made for God, how can the world fill it? If the ocean can be still with miles of unstable waters beneath it, then the soul of man, rocking itself upon its own deep longings, with the Infinite beneath it, may rest. We were created once in majesty, to find enjoyment in God, and if our hearts are empty now, there is nothing for it but to fill up the hollowness of the soul with God.

Let not that expression—filling the soul with God— pass away without a distinct meaning. God is Love and Goodness. Fill the soul with goodness, and fill the soul with love, *that* is the filling it with God. If we love one another, God dwells in us. There is nothing else that can satisfy.

When people of this world grow weary of this phantom chase of life, when they grow sick of gaieties and tired of toil, they will acknowledge that they cannot drink from the fount of blessedness. Instead, they turn aside, either out of broken-heartedness or wisdom, to the pursuit of new expectations even at 50, 60, or 70 years of age. When we see this, we know that we are observing a soul who has a capacity for high and noble things—even for the banquet table of God Himself. Yet he is trying to fill his infinite hollowness with husks.

Once more, there is degradation in the life of irreligion. The things that the wanderer tried to live on were not husks only. They were husks that the swine did eat. Degradation means the application of a thing to purposes lower than that for which it was intended. It is degradation to a man to live on husks, because these are not his true food. We call it degradation when we see the members of an ancient family, decayed by extravagance, working for their bread. It is not degradation for a born laborer to work for an honest livelihood. It is degradation for them, for they are not what they might have been. And therefore, for a man to be degraded, it is not necessary that he should have given himself up to low and mean practices. It is quite enough that he is living for purposes lower than those for which God intended him. He may be a man of unblemished reputation, and yet debased in the truest meaning of the word.

We were sent into this world to love God and to love man; to do good—to fill up life with deeds of generosity and usefulness. He who refuses to work out that high destiny is a degraded man. He may turn away revolted from everything that is gross. His sensuous indulgences may be all marked by refinement and taste. His house may be filled with elegance. His library may be adorned with books. There may be sounds in his mansion that can regale the ear, delicacies that can stimulate the palate, and forms of beauty that can please the eye. There may be nothing in his whole life to offend the most chastened and fastidious delicacy; yet, if the history of all this be, powers which were meant for eternity frittered upon time, the man is degraded—if the spirit which was created to find its enjoyment in the love of God has settled down satisfied with the love of the world, then, just as surely as the sensualist of this parable, that man has turned aside from a celestial feast to prey on garbage.

The Repentance of a Sinner

We pass on to the second period of the history of God's treatment of a sinner. It is the period of his coming to himself, or what we call repentance. The first fact of religious experience that this parable suggests to us is that common truth—men desert the world when the world deserts them. The renegade came to himself when there were no more husks to eat. He would have remained away if he could have got them, but it is written, "no man gave unto him" (Luke 15:16). And this, brethren, is the record of our shame. Invitation is not enough; we must be driven to God. And the famine comes not by chance. God sends the famine into the soul—the hunger, and thirst, and the disappointment—to bring back his erring child again.

The world likes to fasten on that truth and get out of it a triumphant sarcasm against religion. They tell us that just as the caterpillar passes into the chrysalis, and the chrysalis into the butterfly, so profligacy passes into disgust, and disgust passes into religion. To use their own phraseology, when people become disappointed with the world, it is the last resource they say, to turn saint. So the men of the world speak, and they think they are profoundly philosophical and concise in the account they give. The world is welcome to its very small sneer. It is the glory of our Master's gospel that it *is* the refuge of the brokenhearted. It is the strange mercy of our God that He does not reject the writings of a jaded heart.

Let the world curl its lip if it will, when it sees through the causes of the prodigal's return. And if the sinner does not come to God taught by this disappointment, what then? If affections crushed in early life have driven one man to God; if wrecked and ruined hopes have made another man religious; if want of success in a profession has broken the spirit; if the human life lived out too passionately, has left a surfeit and a craving behind which end in seriousness; if one is brought by the sadness of widowed life, and another by the forced desolation of involuntary single life; if when the mighty famine comes into the heart, and not a husk is left, not a pleasure untried, then, and not till then, the remorseful resolve is made, "I will arise and go to my Father"—Well, brethren, what then? Why this, that the history of penitence, produced as it so often is by mere disappointment, sheds only a brighter luster round the love of Christ, who rejoices to receive such wanderers, worthless as they are, back into His bosom.

Thank God the world's sneer is true. It *is* the last resource to turn saint. Thanks to our God that when this gaudy world has ceased to charm, when the heart begins to feel its hollowness, and the world has lost its satisfying power, still all is not yet lost if penitence and Christ remain, to still, to humble, and to soothe a heart which sin has fevered.

There is another truth contained in this section of the parable. After a life of wild sinfulness, religion is servitude at first, not freedom. Observe, he went back to duty with the feelings of a slave: "I am no more worthy to be called thy son, make me as one of thy hired servants" (15:19). Anyone who has lived in the excitement of the world and then tried to settle down at once to quiet duty knows how true that is. To borrow a metaphor from Israel's desert life, it is a tasteless thing to live on manna after you have been feasting upon quails. It is a dull, cold drudgery to find pleasure in simple occupation when life has been a succession of strong emotions. Sonship it is not; it is slavery. A son obeys in love, entering heartily into his father's meaning. A servant obeys mechanically, rising early because he must; perhaps doing his duty well, but feeling in all its force the irksomeness of the service. Sonship does not come all at once. The yoke of Christ is easy, the burden of Christ is light; but it is not light to everybody. It is light when you love it, and no man who has sinned much can love it all at once.

Therefore, if I speak to anyone who is trying to be religious, and heavy in heart because his duty is done too formally, my Christian brother, fear not. You are returning, like the prodigal, with the feelings of a servant. Still it is a real return. The spirit of adoption will come afterward. You will often have to do duties which you cannot relish, and in which you see no meaning.

So it was with Naaman at the prophet's command. He bathed, not knowing why he was bidden to bathe in Jordan. When you bend to prayer, often and often you will have to kneel with wandering thoughts and constraining lips to repeat words into which your heart scarcely enters. You will have to perform duties when the heart is cold, and without a spark of enthusiasm to warm you. But my Christian brother, onward still.

Struggle to the Cross, even though it be struggling as in chains. Just as on a day of clouds, when you have watched the distant hills, dark and gray with mist, suddenly a gleam of sunshine passing over reveals to you, in that flat surface, valleys and dells and spots of sunny happiness, which slept before unsuspected in the fog, so in the gloom of penitential life there will be times when God's deep peace and love will be felt shining into the soul with supernatural refreshment. Let the penitent be content with the servant's lot at first. Liberty and peace, and the bounding sensations of a Father's arms around you, come afterwards.

The Reception of the Prodigal

The last circumstance in this division of our subject is the reception which a sinner meets with on his return to God. "Bring forth the best robe and put it on him, and put a ring on his hand, and shoes on his feet, and bring hither the fatted calf and kill it, and let us eat and be merry" (15:22, 23).

This banquet represents two things. It tells of the father's gladness on his son's return. That represents God's joy on the reformation of a sinner. It tells of a banquet and a dance given to the long lost son. That represents the sinner's gladness when he first understood that God was reconciled to him in Christ.

There is a strange, almost wild, rapture, a strong gush of love and happiness in those days that are called the days of first conversion. When a man who has sinned much—a profligate—turns to God, and it becomes first clear to his apprehension that there is love instead of spurning for him, there is a luxury of emotion—a banquet of tumultuous blessedness in the moment of first love to God, which stand alone in life, nothing before and nothing after like it. And brethren, let us observe: This forgiveness is a thing granted while a man is yet afar off. We are not to wait for the right of being happy till we are good: we might wait forever. Joy is not delayed till we deserve it. Just so soon as a sinful man trusts that the mercy of God in Christ has done away with his transgression, the ring, and the robe, and the shoes are his, the banquet and the light of a Father's countenance.

The Reaction of the Brother

Lastly, we have to consider very briefly God's expostulation with a saint. There is another brother mentioned in this parable, who expressed something like indignation at the treatment which his brother met with. There are commentators who have imagined that this personage represents the Pharisees who complained that Jesus was receiving sinners. But this is manifestly impossible, because his father expostulates with him in this language, "Son, thou art ever with me;" not for one moment could that be true of the Pharisees. The true interpretation seems to be that this elder brother represents a real Christian perplexed with God's mysterious dealings. We have before us the description of one of those happy persons who has been filled with the Holy Spirit from his mother's womb, and on the whole (with imperfections of course) remained God's servant all his life. For this is his own account of himself, which the father does not contradict. "Lo! these many years do I serve thee" (v. 29).

We observe then: The objection made about the reception given a notorious sinner: "Thou never gavest me a kid" (v. 29). Now, in this we have a fact true to Christian experience. Joy seems to be felt more vividly and more exuberantly by men who have sinned much, than by men who have grown up consistently from childhood with religious education. Rapture belongs to him whose sins, which are forgiven, are many. In the perplexity which this fact occasions, there is a feeling that is partly right and partly wrong. There is a surprise that is natural. There is a resentful jealousy that is to be rebuked.

There is first of all a natural surprise. It was natural that the elder brother should feel perplexed and hurt. When a sinner seems to be rewarded with more happiness than a saint, it appears as if good and evil

were alike undistinguished in God's dealings. It seems
like putting a reconciled enemy over the head of a
tried servant. It looks as if it were a kind of encouragement held out to sin, and a man begins to feel, Well if
this is to be the caprice of my father's dealing; if this
rich feast of gladness be the reward of a licentious life,
"Verily, I cleaned my heart in vain, and washed my
hands in innocency" (Ps. 73:13). This is natural surprise.

But besides this, there is a jealousy in these
sensations of ours which God sees fit to rebuke. You
have been trying to serve God all your life, and you
find it struggle and heaviness and dullness still. You
see another who has outraged every obligation of life,
and he is not tried by the deep prostration you think
he ought to have. He seems bright with happiness at
once. You have been making sacrifices all your life,
and your worst trials come out of your most generous
sacrifices. Your errors in judgment have been followed
by sufferings sharper than those that crime itself could
have brought. And you see men who never made a
sacrifice unexposed to trial—men whose life has been
joyous purchased by the ruin of others' innocence—
tasting first the pleasures of sin, and then the banquet
of religion.

You have been a moral man from childhood, and yet
with all your efforts you feel the crushing conviction
that it has never once been granted you to win a soul
to God. And you see another man marked by
inconsistency and impetuosity, banqueting every day
upon the blest success of impressing and saving souls.
All that is startling. And then comes sadness and
despondency; then come all those feelings that are so
graphically depicted here: irritation—"he was angry;"
swelling pride—"he would not go in;" jealousy, which
required soothing—"his father went out and entreated
him."

And now brethren, notice the father's answer. It does
not account for this strange dealing by God's
sovereignty. It does not cut the knot of the difficulty,

instead of untying it, by saying, God has a *right* to do what He will. He does not urge, God has a right to act on favoritism if He please. But it assigns two reasons. The first reason is, "It was fitting that we should make merry" (Luke 15:32). It is fitting that God should be glad on the reclamation of a sinner. It is fitting that that sinner, looking down into the dreadful chasm over which he had been tottering, should feel a shudder of delight through all his frame on thinking of his escape. And it is fitting that religious men should not feel jealous of one another, but freely and generously join in thanking God that others have got happiness, even if *they* have not. The spirit of religious exclusiveness, which looks down contemptuously instead of tenderly on worldly men, and banishes a man for ever from the circle of its joys because he has sinned notoriously, is a bad spirit.

Finally, the reason given for this dealing is, "Son, thou art always with Me, and all that I have is thine" (v. 31). By which Christ seems to tell us that the disproportion between man and man is much less than we suppose. The profligate had had one hour of ecstacy—the other had had a whole life of peace. A consistent Christian may not have ecstacy; but he has that which is much better than pleasure: calmness—God's serene and perpetual presence. And after all brethren, that is the best. One to whom much is forgiven, has much joy. He must have it, if it were only to support him through those fearful trials which are to come—those haunting reminiscences of a polluted heart—those frailties—those inconsistencies to which the habit of past indulgence have made him liable. A terrible struggle is in store for him yet. Grudge him not one hour of unclouded exultation.

Religion's best gift—rest, serenity—the quiet daily love of one who lives perpetually with his Father's family—uninterrupted usefulness—*that* belongs to him who has lived steadily, and walked with duty, neither grieving nor insulting the Holy Spirit of his God. The man who serves God early has the best of it; joy is well in its way, but a few flashes of joy are trifles in comparison with a life of peace. Which is best: the flash of joy lighting up the whole heart, and then darkness till the next flash comes—or the steady calm sunlight of day in which men work?

An Appeal to Prodigals

And now, one word to those who are living this young man's life—thinking to become religious as he did, when they have got tired of the world. I speak to those who are leading a worldly life. Young brethren, let two motives be urged earnestly upon your attention. The first is the motive of mere honorable feeling. We will say nothing about the uncertainty of life. We will not dwell upon this fact, that impressions resisted now, may never come back again. We will not appeal to terror. That is not the weapon a Christian minister loves to use. If our lips were clothed with thunder, it is not denunciation which makes men Christians. Let the appeal be made to every high and generous feeling in a young man's bosom.

Deliberately and calmly you are going to do *this:* to spend the best and most vigorous portion of your days in idleness—in uselessness—in the gratification of self— in the contamination of others. And then weakness, the relics, and the miserable dregs of life—you are going to give *that* sorry offering to God, because His mercy endureth forever! Shame—shame upon the heart that can let such a plan rest in one moment. If it be there, crush it like a man. It is a degrading thing to enjoy husks till there is no man to give them. It is a base thing to resolve to give to God as little as possible, and not to serve Him till you must.

Young brethren, I speak principally to you. You have health for God now. You have strength of mind and body. You have powers that may fit you for real usefulness. You have appetites for enjoyment that can be consecrated to God. You acknowledge the law of honor. Well then, by every feeling of manliness and generosity remember this: now, and not later, is your time to learn what religion means.

There is another motive, and a very solemn one, to be urged upon those who are delaying. Every moment of delay adds bitterness to after struggles. The moment of a feeling of hired servitude must come. If a man will not obey God with a warm heart, he may hereafter have to do it with a cold one. To be holy is the work of a long life. The experience of ten thousand lessons teaches only a little of it; and all this, the work of becoming like God, the man who delays is crowding into the space of a few years, or a few months. When we have lived long a life of sin, do we think that repentance and forgiveness will obliterate all the traces of sin upon the character? Be sure that every sin pays its price: "Whatsoever a man soweth, that shall he also reap" (Gal. 6:7).

Oh! there are recollections of past sin that come crowding up to the brain, with temptation in them. There are old habits that refuse to be mastered by a few enthusiastic sensations. There is so much of the old man clinging to the penitent who has waited long—he is so much as a religious man, like what he was when he was a worldly man—that it is doubtful whether he ever reaches in this world the full stature of Christian manhood. Much warm earnestness but strange inconsistencies—that is the character of one who is an old man and a young Christian. Brethren, do we wish to risk all this? Do we want to learn holiness with terrible struggles, and sore affliction, and the plague of much remaining evil? Then *wait* before you turn to God.

Refusing to Go In

George H. Morrison (1866-1928) assisted the great Alexander Whyte in Edinburgh, pastored two churches, and then became pastor in 1902 of the distinguished Wellington Church on University Avenue in Glasgow. His preaching drew great crowds; in fact, people had to line up an hour before the services to be sure to get seats in the large auditorium. Morrison was a master of the use of imagination in preaching; yet his messages are solidly biblical.

From his many published volumes of sermons, I have chosen this message from *The Afterglow of God,* published in 1912 by Hodder and Stoughton, London.

9

REFUSING TO GO IN

And he was angry, and would not go in (Luke 15:28).

I HAVE OFTEN spoken on this beautiful parable, and I hope often to speak on it again. It is so full of teaching and so full of hope that in a lifetime one could not exhaust it. I think I have even spoken on this verse to you when discussing our duties to our equals. But tonight I choose it for a different purpose, and I want to put it in a different setting. I want to look at the brother in the parable and a type of the man who will not enter into a love that is too big for earth, and into a household that is home indeed.

"And he was angry, and would not go in." Are there not multitudes in that condition? They see the gleaming of the lights of home, and there is the sound of music in their ears. Yet, though they know that they would have a welcome, and even add to the gladness of the home by entering, somehow or other, like the brother here, they stand in the cold night outside the door.

I am not speaking tonight to those who have accepted Christ and know His fellowship. I am speaking to those so near to door and window that they see the light and hear the sound of music. Yet though the night is over them and around them, and they are hungry and the feast is there, somehow or other they will not go in. Let me ask you in passing to lay this to heart, that no one will ever force you in. God is too careful of our human freedom to drag us against our will into His home. You must go willingly or not at all. You must make up your mind to go, and do it. And probably there is no hour so fit for that as just this hour which you have reached tonight.

There are two things about which I want to speak in connection with the conduct of this brother. First, I want to look at the reasons which kept him from entering the home that night. Second, I want to find out what he missed because he thus refused to enter.

Why Did He Refuse?

First, then, looking at the man, why was it that he refused to enter? I think to begin with, this was in his heart: *He could not understand his father's ways.* Doubtless he had always loved his father. Doubtless he had always honored him. He had never before questioned his sagacity or dreamed of thinking of him as unjust. But now, in the hour of the prodigal's return, when the house was ablaze with light and loud with merriment, all he had cherished of his father's justice seemed to be scattered to the winds of heaven. Was *this* the way to receive back a prodigal? Was not this to put a premium on folly? Was it fair to him, so faithful and so patient, that a reckless ne'er-do-well should have this welcome? He could not understand his father's ways.

Is this the only man who has stood outside because of irritating thought like that? Are there none here who will not enter because they cannot understand the Father's dealings? They cannot fathom the mysteries of providence. They cannot understand the cruelties of nature. They cannot grasp the meaning of the cross or see the power of the death of Jesus. Am I speaking to anyone who feels like that—who cannot understand the Father's dealings? I want to say to you that the one way to learn them is to come at once into the home. For the ways of God are like cathedral windows that are dim and meaningless outside, and only reveal their beauty and their story to those who are within.

I also think this man refused to enter because *he was indignant with his brother*. He was indignant that one with such a character should have a place at all within the house. It is not likely that he ever loved his brother, and perhaps his brother had never much loved him. There was such a difference between their natures that they could hardly have been the best of friends.

The one was always generous to a fault and always getting into trouble somewhere. The other was a pattern of sobriety and was as cautious as he was laborious.

Such Jacobs, and they are found in every region, are always a little contemptuous of Esaus. Secretly they despise them and their singing, and they cannot understand why people love them. And when they find that they are home again, and that all the household is in revelry, then are they angry and will not go in. So was it with this person in the parable. He was not only angry with his father, but he was also deeply indignant that in the house of gladness a man such as his brother would be tolerated. And I know many who are standing out—who are angry and will not go in—for a reason similar to that. I remember a young man coming to me in Dundee to tell me why he would never join the church. It seemed that in the place of business where he worked there was a young woman who made a great profession of being a Christian. All the time that she was busy in attending meetings and acting as a monitor, she was pilfering the till. *"And he was angry, and would not go in."* He was very indignant with her. He said, "If these are the kind of people who are *in*, then it is better that I should be *without*. I tell you there are many more just like that who would come in and get their welcome if it were not for what they have seen in you—if it were not for what they have seen in me.

My brother, standing there in the darkness, there is a great deal to justify your attitude. But why do you leave the happiness to *us* when we are such prodigals and so unworthy of it? Come in yourself tonight out of the cold. Bring your enthusiasm and your courage with you. Not only will you receive a blessing, but you will also be a blessing to us all.

I think also that this man refused to enter because *he trusted the reports of others.* He did what is always foolish to do—he went on the information of the servants. Had he gone right in and seen things for himself, the night for him would have had a different appearance. One look at his brother might have softened him, there were such traces of hell about his face. But instead of that he went to the stable door, where the ostler was loafing and listening to the music, and he, the firstborn of his father's family, was content to get his information *there*.

Now, of course we know that he was told the truth. "Thy brother is come, and they are making merry." But might not the truth be told in such a way as would irritate and rankle just a little? It is always the prodigals whom the servants love. It is always the prodigals they like to serve. And there would be just a touch of pleasing malice in it, when they told the elder brother what had happened. *"And he was angry, and would not go in."* It was partly the servants' tone that made him angry. He took his report of that most glorious night from men who knew nothing of its inner mystery.

It is often so, and there are multitudes outside today because they have taken the report of others who are incapable of judging rightly. Are you quite sure that your reports of Jesus are taken from those who know Him and who love Him? Are you quite sure that in your thoughts of Christ there is no travesty of what is true? You must especially beware of that, young man, in an age like this when every one is talking, and when a thousand judgments are passed on Jesus Christ by men who have never touched His garments' hem. I beg of you to believe that in the gospel there is something that lies beyond the reach of intellect. There is something that is never understood except by those who have experienced it. Therefore, if you are in earnest and are wise, you will take no verdict upon the cross of Christ, except the verdict of the man or woman who has experienced its saving power.

What the Brother Missed

To begin, you must all agree with me that *the man missed just what he most needed.* Think of it. His day's work was over. He was coming home in the evening from the field. Like a faithful servant he had been hard at work, driving the furrow or building up the fences. I honor him for that quiet and steady toil and for being not above the servant's duty. There would be more prosperous farms and prosperous businesses, if sons today would follow his example.

Now the labors of the day were over, and he was hungry and he needed food. He was weary and he needed rest. He was soiled and stained with his day's work, and he wanted a change of raiment in the evening—and all that he needed in that evening hour was stored and treasured in his father's house. *"And he was angry, and would not go in."* He missed the very things that he was needing. All that would freshen him and make him strong again, he lost because he stayed outside the door. He was a soiled, weary, and hungry man, and everything was ready for the taking. Yet no one forced him to take it when he deliberately stood outside.

Is not that always the pity of it, when a man refuses the love of Jesus Christ? Is he not missing just what he most needs, and needs the more, the more He has been faithful? For all of us are soiled and we need cleansing. All of us are weak and we need strength. All of us are hungering and thirsting, and Christ alone can satisfy that hunger. My brother and sister, I want you to come in, not to please me, but for your own sake first. I want you to come in because tonight just what you need is waiting for you in Christ. I want you to come in because that heart of yours is restless and unsatisfied and hungry; because when you were tempted last you fell, and you are missing the very thing you need.

Not only did the man miss what he needed, but he also *missed the merriment and gladness.* He missed what some folk would not miss for anything—he missed an excellent dance and a good supper. Think of him, standing out under the stars, a man alone and out of touch with everybody. (Have not you felt it when there was some fine gathering, and you were not one of the invited?) And then, to make it worse for the son to bear, the sound of the music floated through the yard, and he could see how happy they all were as the figures passed beyond the lighted window. The man was bitten by the fiercest jealousy. He was hurt. He was offended. He was miserable. Everyone was joyous except him. Everyone was in the light but he. And the strange thing is that in all the countryside there was not a man who would have been more welcome, nor one who had a better right and title to the gladness and the feasting of the night.

Ah! what a right some of you have to know the joy and feasting of the Lord! How you have been prayed for since you were little children! How hearts at home have yearned for you in tears! And yet today you are the very one—you who have had an upbringing like that—who stand outside and will not enter in. You miss the gladness of the Lord Jesus Christ. I want you to come right in tonight. You are far more lonely than some people think. I want you to have the gladness of religion, instead of your little petty evanescent gladness. I want you to feel that in the love of Christ, with all its strengthening and all its saving, there is just that deep, strong joy that you are missing and always will miss till you pass through the door.

Then tell me, did he not miss one thing more? *Did he not miss his chance of making others happy?* Although I daresay he never thought it so, his absence was the one shadow on that feast. He was not, I take it, a very lovable person, and for that matter perhaps you are not either. He was not at all the kind of man who is the life and soul of any gathering. And yet that night—that night and that alone—*his* presence would have been the crowning gladness; his absence was the one dark shadow upon a happiness that was like that of heaven. Do you think the prodigal could be at peace until his brother had come in and welcomed him? Could the father be happy when there was one so unhappy? One he loved and honored for his toil? And all the time, bitter and angry-hearted, the man outside was missing his great chance, a chance that it is worth living years to win—the chance of making other people happy.

Have you ever thought, young men and women, of the happiness you would give by coming in? If you have never thought of it before, I want you to think of it today. What of your mother, who has toiled and prayed for you? What of your father, though he never says much? What of that friend whose eyes would be so different if you were but a faithful soul in Christ? What of the angels in their ranks and choirs who are waiting to rejoice when you are saved? What of Jesus Christ, the lover of mankind, who would see of the travail of His soul and would be satisfied? I beg of you not to miss your opportunity. It is a great vocation to make others glad. I would call you to it even if it were hard, and even if it meant that sacrifice to what was most dear. But the wonderful thing about our Lord is this, that when you trust Him, and make others glad, in that very hour you become glad yourself, and win what you have craved all along.

The Reception of Sinners

Charles Haddon Spurgeon (1834-1892) is undoubtedly the most famous minister of modern times. Converted in 1850, he united with the Baptists and very soon began to preach in various places. He became pastor of the Baptist church in Waterbeach in 1851, and three years later he was called to the decaying Park Street Church, London. Within a short time, the work began to prosper, a new church was built and dedicated in 1861, and Spurgeon became London's most popular preacher. In 1855, he began to publish his sermons weekly; and today they make up the fifty-seven volumes of *The Metropolitan Tabernacle Pulpit*. He founded a pastor's college and several orphanages.

This sermon is taken from *The Metropolitan Tabernacle Pulpit*, volume 20. Spurgeon preached it at The Tabernacle on Sunday morning, November 22, 1874.

10

THE RECEPTION OF SINNERS

But the father said to his servants, Bring forth the best robe, and put it on him; and put a ring on his hand, and shoes on his feet: And bring the fatted calf, and kill it; and let us eat and be merry (Luke 15:22, 23).

LAST LORD'S DAY we spoke about the consecration of priests. That theme might seem too high for troubled hearts and trembling consciences, who fear that they will never be made priests and kings unto God. Such a glorious privilege appears to them to hang in the dim, distant future—if indeed they reach it at all. Therefore, at this time, we will go down from the elevated regions to comfort those who are seeking the Lord, with the view of helping them to climb also.

We speak this morning, not of the consecration of priests, but of the reception of sinners. This, according to our text, is a very joyful business. It is even described as a merrymaking, accompanied with music and with dancing. We frequently speak of the sorrow for sin that accompanies conversion, and I do not think we can speak of it too often; yet there is a possibility of our overlooking the equally holy and remarkable joy that attends the return of a soul to God.

It has been a common error to suppose that a man must pass through a considerable time of despondency—if not of horror of mind—before he can find peace with God. Now in this parable the father seems determined to cut short that period. He stops his son in the very middle of his confession, and before he can ask to be made as one of the hired servants, his mournful style is changed for rejoicing, for the father has already fallen on his neck and kissed his trembling lips into a sweet silence.

It is not the Lord's desire that sinners should tarry

long in the state of unbelieving conviction of sin. It is something wrong in themselves that keeps them there. Either they are ignorant of the freeness and fulness of Christ or they harbor self-righteous hope or they cling to their sins. Sin lieth at the door; it is no work of God which blocks the way. God delights in their delight, and joys in their joy. It is the Father's will that the penitent sinner should at once believe in Jesus, at once find complete forgiveness, and immediately enter into rest.

If any of you came to Jesus without the dreary interval of terror that is so frequent, I pray you do not judge yourselves as though your conversions were dubious—they are all the more instead of all the less genuine because they bear rather the marks of the gospel than of the law. The weeping of Peter, which in a few days turns to joy, is far better than the horror of Judas, which ends in suicide. Conversions, as recorded in Scripture, are for the most part exceedingly rapid. They were pricked in the heart at Pentecost, and the same day they were baptized and added to the church, because they had found peace with God through Jesus Christ. Paul was smitten down with conviction, and in three days was a baptized believer.

Perhaps the illustration is not complete, but I was about to say that sometimes God's power is so very near us that the lightning flash of conviction is often attended at the very same moment by the deep thunder of the Lord's voice, which drives away our fears and proclaims peace and pardon to the soul. In many cases the sharp needle of the law is immediately followed by the silken thread of the gospel; the showers of repentance are succeeded at once by the sunshine of faith; peace overtakes penitence, and walks arm in arm with her into yet fuller rest.

Having thus reminded you that God would have penitents very soon rejoice, I want to spend this morning in setting forth the joy that is caused by pardoned sin. That joy is threefold. We will talk about it first as *the joy of God over sinners;* second, *the joy of sinners in God;* and, third, what is so often forgotten, *the joy of the servants,* for they too rejoiced, for the father said, "Let *us* eat and be merry." One of the point of the parable is just this, that as in the case of the lost sheep the shepherd called together his friends and neighbors, and as in the case of the piece of money the woman called her neighbors together, so in this case, also, others share in the joy that chiefly belongs to the loving father and the returning wanderer.

The Joy of God Over Sinners

It is always difficult to speak of the ever-blessed God appropriately when we have to describe Him as touched by emotions. I pray, therefore, to be guided in my speech by the Holy Spirit. We have been educated into the idea that the Lord is above emotions, either of sorrow or pleasure. That He cannot suffer, for instance, is always laid down as a self-evident postulate. Is that quite so clear? Cannot He do or bear anything He chooses to do? What means the Scripture which says that man's sin before the flood made the Lord repent that He had made man on the earth, "and it grieved him at his heart"? (Gen. 6:6). Is there no meaning in the Lord's own language, "Forty years long was I grieved with this generation"? Are we not forbidden to grieve the Holy Spirit? Is He not described as having been vexed by ungodly men! Surely, then, He can be grieved: it cannot be an altogether meaningless expression.

For my part, I rejoice to worship the living God, who, because He is living, does grieve and rejoice. It makes one feel more love to Him than if He dwelt on some serene Olympus, careless of all our woes, because He were incapable of any concern about us, or interest in us, one way or the other. To look upon Him as utterly impassive and incapable of anything like emotion does not, to my mind, exalt the Lord, but rather brings Him down to be comparable to the gods of stone or wood, which cannot sympathize with their worshipers. No, Jehovah is not insensible. He is the living God, and everything that goes with life—pure, perfect holy life—is to be found in Him. Such a subject must always be spoken of very tenderly, with solemn awe.

Although we know something of what God is, for we are made in the image of God, and the best likeness of God undoubtedly was man as he came from his Maker's hand, yet man is not God, and even in his perfectness he must have been a very tiny miniature of God. And now that he has sinned he has blotted and blurred that image.

The finite cannot fully mirror the infinite, nor can the grand, glorious, essential properties of deity be communicated to creatures. They must remain peculiar to God alone. The Lord is, however, continually represented as displaying joy. Moses declared to sinful Israel that if they returned and obeyed the voice of the Lord, the Lord would again rejoice over them for good, as He rejoiced over their fathers (Deut. 30:9). The Lord is said to rejoice in His works and to delight in mercy, and surely we must believe it. Wherefore should we doubt it? Many passages of Scripture speak very impressively of God's joy in His people. Zephaniah put it in the strongest manner: "He will save, He will rejoice over thee with joy; He will rest in His love, He will joy over thee with singing" (3:17). Our God is forever the happy or blessed God; we cannot think of Him as other than supremely blessed. Still, from the Scriptures we gather that He displays on certain occasions a special joy which He would have us recognize. I do not think that it can be mere parable; it is real fact: The Lord *does* rejoice over returning and repenting sinners.

Every being manifests its joy according to its nature and seeks means for its display suitable to itself. It is so with men. When the old Romans celebrated a triumph because some great general returned a victor from Africa, Greece, or Asia with the spoils of a long campaign, how did the fierce Roman nature express its joy? Why, in the Colosseum, or in some yet vaster amphitheater, where buzzing nations choked the ways. They gathered in their myriads to behold not only beasts, but their fellow men, "butchered to make a Roman holiday." Cruelty upon an extraordinary scale was their way of expressing the joy of their iron hearts. Look at the self-indulgent man! He has had a prosperous season and has made a lucky hit, as he calls it, or some event has occurred in his family that makes him very jubilant. What will he do to show forth his joy? Will he bow the knee in gratitude, or lift a hymn of praise? Not he. He will hold a drinking bout. And when he and his fellows are mad with wine, his joy will find expression! The sensual show their joy by sensuality.

Now God, whose name is good and whose nature is love, when He has joy expresses it in mercy, in lovingkindness, and grace. The father's joy in the parable before us showed itself in the full forgiveness accorded, in the kiss of perfect love bestowed, in the gift of the best robe, the ring, and the sandals, and in the gladsome festival that filled the whole house with hallowed mirth. Everything expresses its joy according to its nature. Infinite love, therefore, reveals its joy in acts of love.

The nature of God being as much above ours as the heaven is above the earth, the expression of His joy is therefore all the loftier, and His gifts the greater. Still, there is a likeness between God's way of expressing joy and ours, which it will be profitable to note. *How do we express ourselves, ordinarily, when we are glad? We do so very commonly by a display of bounty.* When in the olden time our kings came into the city of London, or a great victory was celebrated, the conduit in Cheapside ran with red wine, and even the gutters flowed with it. Then were there tables set in the street, and my lords, and the aldermen, and the mayor kept open house, and everybody was fed to the full. Joy was expressed by hospitality.

You have seen the picture of the young heir coming of age, and have noticed how the artist depicts the great yard of the manor-house as full of men and women, who are eating and drinking to their hearts' content. At Christmas seasons, and upon marriage days and harvest homes, men ordinarily express their joy by bountiful provision. So also does the father in this wondrous parable exhibit the utmost bounty, representing thereby the boundless liberality of the great Father of spirits, who shows His joy over penitents by the manner in which He entertains them. The best robe, the ring, the shoes, and the fatted calf, and the "Let us eat and be merry," all show by their bountifulness that God is glad. His oxen and his fatlings are killed, for the feast of mercy is the banquet of the Lord. So unrivalled are the gifts of His gracious hand that the receivers of His favors have cried out in amazement, "Who is a God like unto thee!"

Beloved, consider awhile the Lord's bounty to returning sinners, blotting out their sins like a cloud, and like a thick cloud their iniquities, justifying them in the righteousness of Christ, endowing them with His Holy Spirit, regenerating them, comforting them, illuminating them, purifying them, strengthening them, guiding them, protecting them, filling them with all His own fulness, satisfying their mouth with good things, and crowning them with tender mercies. I see in the bounty of God with which He so liberally endows returning sinners a mighty proof that His inmost soul rejoices over the salvation of men.

At glad times men generally manifest some speciality in their bounty. On the day of the young heir's coming of age, the long-stored cask of the wine is opened and the best bullock is roasted whole. So here in the parable we read, *"Bring forth* the best robe," indicating that it had been laid by and kept in store until then. Nobody had used that robe, it was locked up in the wardrobe, only to be brought out on some very special occasion. This was the happiest day that ever had made glad the house, and therefore "Bring forth the best robe," no other will suffice. Meat is wanted for the banquet. Let a calf be killed. Which shall it be? A calf taken at random from the herd? No, but *the fatted* calf which has been standing in the stalls, and is well-fed, and has been reserved for a festival.

Oh, beloved, when God blesses a sinner, He shows His joy be giving him the reserved mercies, the *special* treasures of everlasting love, the precious things of grace, the secret of the covenant: yea, He has given to sinners the best of the best in giving them Christ Jesus, and the indwelling of the Holy Spirit. The best that heaven affords God bestows on sinners when they come to Him. No scraps and odds and ends are dealt out to hungry and thirsty seekers, but in princely munificence of unstinting love the heavenly Father deals out abundant grace. I would that sinners would come and try my Lord's hospitality; they would find His table to be more richly loaded than even that of Solomon, though thirty oxen and a hundred sheep did not suffice for one day's provision for the household of that magnificent sovereign. If they would but come, even the largest-hearted among them would be wonder-struck as they saw how richly God supplied all their need, according to His riches in glory by Christ Jesus.

> Rags exchanged for costly treasure,
>   Shoes and ring and heaven's best robe!
> Gifts of *love* which knows no measure;
>   Who can tell the heart of God?
> All his loved ones—his redeemed ones,
>   Perfect are in his abode.

We also show our joy by a concentration of thought upon the object of it. When a man is carried away with joy he forgets everything else, and gives himself up to the one delight. David was so glad to bring back the Ark of the Lord that he danced before the Lord with all his might, being clad only with a linen ephod. He laid aside his stately garments and thought so little of his dignity that Michal sneered at him. He was so much absorbed in adoring his Lord that all regard to appearances was quite gone. Observe well the parable, and think you hear the father say, "Bring forth the best robe and put it on *him,* and put a ring on *his* hand and shoes on *his* feet, and let us eat and be merry, for *this my son* was dead and is alive again." The son alone is in the father's eye, and the whole house must be ordered in reference to him. Nothing is to be thought of today but the long-lost son. He is paramount in the wardrobe, the jewel room, the farmyard, the kitchen, and the banqueting chamber. He that was lost, he that was dead, he being found and alive, engrosses the whole of the father's mind.

Sinner, it is wonderful how God sets all His thoughts on you according to His promise, "I will set mine eyes upon them for good" (Jer. 24:6); and again, "I will watch over them, to build and to plant, saith the Lord" (Jer. 31:28). The Lord thinks upon the poor and needy, His eyes are upon them and His ears are open to their cry. He thinks as much of each penitent sinner as if He were the only being in the universe. O penitent, for you is the working of the Lord's providence to bring you home, for you the training of His ministers that they might know how to reach your heart, for you the gifts of the Spirit upon them that they might be powerful with your conscience; yea, for you His Son, His eternal Son once bleeding on the cross, and now sitting in the highest heavens making intercession for you.

I saw in Amsterdam diamond cutting, and I noticed great wheels, a large factory and powerful engines, and all the power was made to bear upon a small stone no larger than the nail of my little finger. All that huge machinery for that little stone, because it was so precious! I see you poor insignificant sinners, who have rebelled against your God, brought back to your Father's house, and now the whole universe is full of wheels and all those wheels are working together for your good, to make out of you a jewel fit to glisten in the Redeemer's crown.

God is not represented as saying more of creation than that "it was very good," but in the work of grace He is described as singing for joy. He breaks the eternal silence and cries, "My son is found." As the philosopher who had compelled nature to yield her secret ran through the street crying, "Eureka! Eureka! I have found it! I have found it!" so does the Father dwell on the word, "my son that was dead, is alive again, he that was lost is found." The whole Scripture aims at the bringing back again of the Lord's banished. For this the Redeemer leaves His glory, for this the church sweeps her house and lights her candle, and when the work is done all other bliss is secondary to the surpassing joy of the Lord, of which He bids His ransomed ones partake, saying, "Enter ye into the joy of your Lord" (Matt. 25:21).

We also show our joy by an alacrity of motion. I quoted David just now. It was so with him, he danced before the ark. I cannot imagine David walking slowly before the ark, or creeping after it like a mourner at a funeral. I often notice the difference between your coming to this place and people going to other places of worship. I remark a very solemn, stately, and somber motion in almost everybody else, but you come tripping along as if you were glad to go up to the house of the Lord. You do not regard the place of our joyous assemblies as a sort of religious prison, but as the palace and banqueting house of the great King.

When anyone is joyous, he is sure to show it by quickness of his motions. Hearken to the father, he says, "Bring forth the best robe and put it on him, and put a ring on his hand, and shoes on his feet, and bring hither the fatted calf, and let us eat and be merry." As quickly as possible he pours out sentence after sentence. There is no delay; no interval between the commands. Might he not have said, "Bring forth the best robe and put it on him, and let us look at him awhile, and sit down and prepare him for the next step. And in an hour's time, or tomorrow, we will put a ring on his hand. Then soon we will put shoes on his feet; he is best without shoes for the present, for perhaps if he has shoes on he will run away. As to the festival, perhaps we had better rejoice over him when we see whether his repentance is genuine." No, no, no, the father's heart is too glad; he must bless his boy at once, heap on his favors, and multiply his tokens of love.

When the Lord receives a sinner, he runs to meet him, he falls on his neck, he kisses him, he speaks to him, he forgives him, he justifies him, he sanctifies him, he puts him among the children, he opens the treasure of his grace to him, and all in quick succession. Within a few minutes after he has been cleansed from sin, the prodigal is robed, adorned, and shod for service. The love of our Redeemer's heart made Him say to the poor thief, "Today shalt thou be with me in Paradise." He would not let him linger in pain on the cross, but carried him away to Paradise in an hour or two. Love and joy are ever quick of foot. God is slow to anger, but He is so plenteous in His mercy that His grace overflows and rushes on like a torrent when it leaps along the ravine.

The joy of the father was also shown as ours often is by open utterance. It is hard for a glad man to hold his tongue. What can dumb people do when they are very happy? I cannot imagine how they endure silence at such times; it must then be a terrible misfortune. When you are very happy you must tell somebody. So does this father. He pours out his joy, and the utterance is very simple. "My son was dead, and is alive again, was lost, and is found." Yet, simple as it it, it is poetry.

The poetry of the Hebrews consisted in parallelism, or a repetition of the sense or a part of the words. Here are two lines that pair with each other, and make a verse of Hebrew poetry. Glad men when they speak naturally and simply always say the right thing in the very best manner, using nature's poetry, as does the father here. Note also that there is reiteration in his utterance. He might have been satisfied to say, "This my son was dead and is alive again." No; the fact is so sweet he must repeat it, "He was lost, and is found." Even thus we speak when we are very full of sweet content; the heart bubbleth up with a good matter, and over again and over again we rehearse our joy. When the morsel is sweet, we roll it under the tongue. We cannot help it.

So the Lord rejoices over sinners, and tells his joy in

holy scripture in varied phrase and metaphor, and though those scriptures are simple in their style, yet they contain the very essence of poetry. The bards of the Bible stand in the first rank amongst the sons of song, God himself deigning to use poetry to utter His joy because a more prosaic manner would be all too cold and tame. Hear how he puts it: "As the bridegroom rejoiceth over the bride, so shall thy God rejoice over thee" (Isa. 62:5). "I will rejoice in Jerusalem and joy in my people." We might have been left in the dark about this joy of God; we might have been coldly informed that God would save sinners, and we might never have known that He found such joy in it; but the divine joy was too great to be concealed, the great heart of God could not restrain itself, He must tell out to all the universe the delight which the exercise of mercy brought to Him. It was proper that He should make merry and be glad, and therefore He did it. Nothing that is proper to be done will ever be neglected by the Lord our God.

Thus, dear friends, have I feebly spoken of the joy of God, and I want you to notice that it is a delight in which every attribute of God takes a share. Condescension ran to meet the son, love fell on his neck, grace kissed him, wisdom clothed him, truth gave him the ring, peace shod him, wisdom provided the feast, and power prepared it. Not one attribute of the divine nature quarrels with the forgiveness and salvation of a sinner; not one attribute holds back from the beloved employ. Power strengthens the weak, and mercy binds up the wounded. Justice smiles upon the justified sinner, for it is satisfied through the atoning blood, and truth puts forth her hand to guarantee that the promise of grace is fulfilled. Immutability confirms what has been done, and omniscience looks around to see that nothing is left undone. The whole of deity is brought to bear upon a poor worm of the dust, to lift it up and transform it into an heir of God, joint-heir with the Only Begotten. The joy of God occupies the whole of His being, so that when we think of it we may well say, "Bless the Lord, O my soul, and all that is within me bless his holy name," since all that is within Him is engaged to bless His saints.

This joy of the Lord should give every sinner great confidence in coming to God by Jesus Christ, for if you would be glad to be saved, He will be glad to save you. If you long to lay your head in your Father's bosom, your Father's bosom longs to have it there. If you pant to say, "I have sinned," He equally longs to say to you, by acts of love, "I forgive thee freely." If you pine to be His child in His own house once more, the door is open, and He himself is on the watch. Come and welcome, come and welcome, and no more delay.

The Joy of the Sinner

The son was glad. He did not express it in words, as far as I can see in the parable, but he felt nonetheless— but all the more. Sometimes silence is discreet, and it was so in this case. At other times it is absolutely forced upon you by inability to utter the emotion, and this also was true of the prodigal. The son's heart was too full for utterance in words, but he had speaking eyes, and a speaking countenance as he looked on that dear father. As he put on the robe, the ring, and the shoes, he must have been too astonished to speak. He wept in showers that day, but the tears were not salt with grief; they were sweet tears, glittering like the dew of the morning. What would make the son glad, think you? Why, the father's love, the father's forgiveness, and restoration to his old place in the father's heart. That was the point.

Each gift would serve as a token of that love and make the joy overflow. There was the *robe* put on—the dress of a son, and of a son well beloved and accepted. Have you noticed how the robe answered to his confession? The sentences match each other thus: "Father, I have sinned" — "Bring forth the best robe and put it on him." Cover all his sins with Christ's righteousness; put away his sin by imputing to him the righteousness of the Lord Jesus. The robe also met his condition; he was in rags, therefore, "Bring forth the best robe and put it on him," and you shall see no more of his rags. It was fit that he should be thus arrayed, in token of his restoration. He who is re-endowed with the privileges of a son should not be dressed in sordid clothes, but wear raiment suitable to his station. Moreover, since a festival was about to begin, he ought to wear a festive garment. It would not be seemly for him to feast and be merry in his rags. Put the best robe on him that he may be ready to take his place at the banquet. So when the penitent comes to God he is not only covered, as to the past, by the righteousness of Christ, but he is prepared for the future blessedness that is reserved for the pardoned ones. Yea, he is filled to begin the rejoicing at once.

Then came the *ring,* a luxury rather than a necessity, except that now that he was a son it was well that he should be restored to all the honors of his relationship. The signet ring in the east in former times conferred great privileges. In those days men did not sign their names, but stamped with their signet upon wax, so that the ring gave a man power over property, and made him a sort of other self to the man whose ring he wore.

The father gives the son a ring, and how complete as answer was that gift to another clause of his confession. Let me read the two sentences together, "I am no more worthy to be called thy son." "Put a ring on his hand." The gift precisely meets the confession. It also tallied with his changed condition. How singular that the very hand that had been feeding swine should now wear a ring. There were no rings on his hands when they were soiled at the trough, I warrant you. But now he is a swine-feeder no longer, but an honored son of a rich father. Slaves wear no rings. Juvenal laughs at certain freed-men because they were seen walking up and down the Via Sacra with conspicuous rings on their fingers, the emblems of their new found liberty. The ring indicated the penitent's liberty from sin, and his enjoyment of the full privileges of his Father's house.

O, beloved, the Lord will make you glad if you come

to Him. He will put the seal of the Holy Spirit's indwelling upon you, which is both the earnest of the inheritance and the best adornment of the hand of your practical character. You shall have a sure and honorable token, and you shall know that all things are yours, whether things present, or things to come. This ring upon your finger will declare your marriage union to Christ, set forth the eternal love which the Father has fixed upon you, and be the abiding pledge of the perfect work of the Holy Ghost.

Then they put *shoes* on his feet. I suppose he had worn out his own. In the east, servants do not usually wear shoes at home, and especially in the best rooms of the house. The master and the son wear the sandals, but not the servants, so that this order was an answer to the last part of the penitent's prayer, "Make me as one of thy hired servant." "No," says the father, "put shoes on his feet." In the forgiven sinner the awe that puts off its shoes is to be overmatched by the familiarity which wears the shoes which infinite love provides. The forgiven one is no longer to tremble at Sinai, but he is to come unto Mount Zion, and to have familiar intercourse with God. Thus also the restored one was shod for filial service—he could run upon his father's errands or work in his father's fields. He had now in every way all that he could want—the robe that covered him, the ring that adorned him, and the shoe that prepared him for travel or labor.

Now you awakened and anxious ones who are longing to draw near to God, I would that this description of the joy of the prodigal would induce you to come at once. Come, you that see your natural deformity through sin, and He will adorn you with a ring of beauty. Come, you who feel as if you could not come, for you have bleeding, weary feet, and He will shoe you with the silver sandals of His grace. Only do but come, and you shall have such joy in your hearts as you have never dreamed of. There shall be a young heaven born within your spirit, which shall grow and increase until it comes to the fulness of bliss.

The Joy of the Servants

They were to be merry, and they were merry, for the music and the dancing which were heard outside could not have proceeded from one person only. There must have been many to join in it, and who should these be but the servants to whom the father gave his commands? They ate, they drank, they danced, they joined in the music. There are many of us here who are the servants of our own heavenly Father; though we are His children, we delight to be His servants. Now, whenever a sinner is saved, we have our share of joy.

We have joy, first, *in the Father's joy*. They were so glad, because their lord was glad—good servants are always pleased when they see that their master is greatly gratified, and I am sure the Lord's servants are always joyous when they feel that their Lord is well pleased. That servant who went out to the elder brother showed by his language that he was in sympathy with the father, for he pleaded with the son about the matter. When you are in sympathy with God, my dear brother or sister, if the Lord lets you see poor sinners saved, you must and will rejoice with Him. It will be to you better than finding a purse full of money, or making a great gain in business. Yea, nothing in the world can give you more delight than to see some brother of yours or some child of yours made to rejoice in Christ.

A mother once beautifully said, "I remember the new and strange emotions that trembled in my breast when as an infant he was first folded to my heart—my firstborn child. The thrill of that moment still lingers; but when he was "born again," clasped in my arms a "new creature in Christ Jesus," my spiritual child, my son in the gospel, pardoned, justified, adopted, saved, forever saved! Oh! it was the very depth of joy; joy unspeakable! My child was a child of God! The prayers that preceded his birth, that cradled his infancy, and girdled his youth were answered. My son was Christ's. The weary watchings, the yearning desires, the trembling hopes of years were at rest. Our firstborn son was avowedly the Lord's." May every father and mother here know just such a joy by having sympathy with God.

But they had sympathy with *the son.* I am sure they rejoiced to see *him* back again, for somehow usually even bad sons have the goodwill of good servants. When young men go away and are a great grief to their fathers, the servants often stick to them. They will say, "Well, Master John was very inconsiderate and he vexed his father a great deal, but I should like to see the poor boy back again." Especially is this true of the old servants who have been in the house since the boy was born. They never forgot him. And you will find that God's old servants are always glad when they see prodigal children return. They are delighted beyond measure because they love them after all, notwithstanding their wanderings. Sinner, with all your faults and hardness of heart, we do love you, and we should be glad for your sake to see you delivered from eternal ruin and from the wrath of God that now abides on you, and to see you brought to rejoice in pardoned sin and acceptance in the Beloved.

We should rejoice for the sinner's sake, but I think the servants rejoiced most of all when *they were the instruments* in the father's hand of blessing the son. Just look at this. The father said to the servants, "Bring forth the best robe." He might have gone to the wardrobe himself with a key, opened it, and brought out the robe himself. But he gave them the pleasure of doing it. When I get my orders from my Lord and Master on the Lord's day morning to bring forth the best robe, I am delighted indeed. Nothing delights me more than to preach the imputed righteousness of Jesus Christ, and the substitutionary sacrifice of our exalted Redeemer. "Bring forth the best robe." Why, my Master, I might be content to keep out of heaven if thou wouldst always give me this work to do—to bring forth the best robe and extol and exalt Jesus Christ in the eyes of the people.

Then the father said, "Put it on him." When our Lord gives us grace to do that, there is more joy still.

How many times I have brought forth the best robe, but could not put it on you. I have held it up, and expatiated on its excellencies, and pointed to your rags, and said what a delightful thing it would be if I could put it on you, but I could not. But when the heavenly Father, by His divine grace and the power of the Spirit, makes us the means of bringing these treasures into the possession of poor sinners, oh, what joy! I should rejoice to bring forth the ring of the Spirit's sealing work and the shoes of the preparation of the gospel of peace, for it is a joy to exhibit these blessings. And it is a greater joy still to put them on the poor, returning wanderer. God be thanked for giving His servants so great a pleasure! I would not have dared to describe the Lord's servants as putting on the robe, the ring, and the shoes, but as He has Himself done so I am rejoiced to use the Holy Spirit's own language.

How sweet was the command, "Put it on *him*." Yes, put it on the poor trembling, ragged, shivering sinner, "Put it on *him*," even on him, though he can hardly believe such mercy to be possible. "Put it on *him?*" Yes, on *him*. He who was a drunkard, a swearer, an adulterer? Yes, put it on *him*, for he repents. What joy it is when we are enabled by God's commission to throw that glorious mantle over a great sinner. As for the ring, put it on *him;* that is the beauty of it. And the shoes, put them on *him*. That they are for *him* is the essence of our joy—that such a sinner, and especially when he is one of our own household, should receive these gifts of grace is wonderful!

It was most kind of the father to divide the labor of love. One would put on the robe, another the ring, and a third the shoes. Some of my brethren can preach Jesus Christ in His righteousness gloriously, and they put on the best robe; others seem most gifted in dwelling upon the work of the Spirit of God, and they put on the ring. Another class are practical divines, and they put on the shoes. I do not mind which I have to do, if I may but have a part in helping to bring to poor sinners those matchless gifts of grace, which at infinite expense the Lord has prepared for those who come back to Him. How glad those were who helped to dress him I cannot tell.

Meanwhile, another servant was gone off out of doors to bring in the fatted calf, and perhaps two or three were engaged in killing and dressing it, while another was lighting a fire in the kitchen, and preparing the spits for the roast. One laid the table, and another ran to the garden to bring flowers to make wreaths for the room—I know I should have done that if I had been there. All were happy. All ready to join in the music and dancing. Those who work for the good of sinners are always the gladdest when they are saved. You who pray for them, you who teach them, you who preach to them, you who win them for Christ, you shall share their merriment.

Now, dear brethren, we are told that they "began to be merry," and according to the description it would seem that they were merry indeed. But still they only "began." I see no intimation that they ever stopped. "They began to be merry," and as merriment is apt to grow beyond all bounds when it once starts, who knows what they have come to by this time. The saints begin to be merry now, and they will never cease, but rejoice evermore. On earth all the joy we have is only beginning to be merry, it is up in heaven that they get into full swing. Here our best delight is hardly better than a neap tide at its ebb; there the joy rolls along in the majesty of a full spring tide.

> Oh what rapturous hallelujahs
> In our Father's home above!
> Hallelujah! Hallelujah!
> O'er the embraces of his love!
> Wondrous welcome—God's own welcome,
> May the chief of sinners prove.
>
> Sweet melodious strains ascending,
> All around a mighty flood;
> Servants, friends, with joy attending—
> Oh! the happiness of God!
> Grace abounding, all transcending,
> Through a Savior's precious blood.

Let us begin to be merry this morning. But we cannot unless we are laboring for the salvation of others in all ways possible to us. If we have done and are doing that, let us praise and bless the Lord, and rejoice with the reclaimed ones. And let us keep the feast as Jesus would have it kept; for I hope there is no one here of the elder brethren who will be angry and refuse to go in. Let us continue to be merry as long as we live, because the lost are found and the dead are made alive. God grant you to be merry on this account, world without end. Amen.

SCRIPTURE TEXT INDEX

Additional Titles in the *Kregel Classic Sermons* Series

The reading of these sermons will enrich your life, and enhance your skills as an interpreter, teacher, and communicator of God's truth.

CLASSIC SERMONS ON CHRISTIAN SERVICE

Dynamic principles for Christian service will be found in these classic sermons by highly acclaimed pulpit masters. The Christian preacher or teacher will find many exciting insights to instruct and motivate participation in serving others.

CLASSIC SERMONS ON FAITH AND DOUBT

Twelve pulpit giants give you inspiration and devotional challenge for your faith in this book of sermons. These messages to stimulate your faith are from the pulpit ministry of John H. Jowett, D. Martyn Lloyd-Jones, Martin Luther, G. Campbell Morgan, John Wesley and others. Preachers and lay persons alike will be encouraged and find great blessing in these forceful messages.

CLASSIC SERMONS ON OVERCOMING FEAR

One of the overriding problems confronting modern man is the paralyzing effect of fear on the emotions and intellect. The Christian faith has an answer to this problem that provides serenity in the midst of anxiety. Included are sermons by such famous pulpit masters as Hugh Black, V. Raymond Edman, John Henry Jowett, Clarence Edward Nobel Macartney, Alexander Maclaren, G. Campbell Morgan, George H. Morrison, Charles Haddon Spurgeon, and George W. Truett. Preachers and teachers will find *Classic Sermons on Overcoming Fear* a rich resource of positive approaches to the problems of fear.

CLASSIC SERMONS ON PRAYER

Pulpit giants Dwight L Moody, G. Campbell Morgan, Charles H. Spurgeon, R. A. Torrey, Alexander Whyte, and others, present the need, the how-to, and the results of a life that is permeated with prayer. These classic sermons on prayer will energize your prayer life, show you how to expect great things from God, and help you experience the strengthening power of God in your everyday life.

CLASSIC SERMONS ON SUFFERING

Let the pulpit giants provide your resource material for words of comfort and solace. A master preacher in his own right, Warren W.

Wiersbe compiled these sixteen sermons by Phillips Brooks, John Calvin, Walter A. Maier, Charles H. Spurgeon, George W. Truett and others, to offer perspective, understanding, and encouragement for the depressed and brokenhearted.

CLASSIC SERMONS ON WORSHIP

Rediscover the beauty of worship! In this day of renewed appreciation for biblical worship, believers need to hear the resounding voices of some of God's greatest Bible communicators from the past. This exciting collection of *Classic Sermons* will help Christians understand what the Bible says about worship, and will motivate us to apply these vital truths to our lives and churches.

CLASSIC SERMONS ON THE ATTRIBUTES OF GOD

Powerful sermons by highly acclaimed pulpit masters lay a solid foundation for growing in the knowledge of God. Rediscover the profound truths revealed in His attributes, such as His: terribleness and gentleness, mercy, knowability, sovereignty, jealousy, omnipresence, immutability, comfort, greatness, omniscience, and love. You will be inspired and challenged by these great sermons from such famous preachers as: J. D. Jones, George H. Morrison, Dwight L Moody, Henry Ward Beecher, Arthur J. Gossip, John H. Jowett, J. Stuart Holden, Joseph Parker, Frederick W. Robertson, Charles H. Spurgeon, and John Wesley.

CLASSIC SERMONS ON THE BIRTH OF CHRIST

The central theme of the Bible is expanded and expounded in this collection of sermons. These messages from pulpit giants of the past will be a welcome addition to both preachers and teachers and will provide inspiration, ideas, and insights into this important event.

CLASSIC SERMONS ON THE CROSS OF CHRIST

An inspiring collection of sermons on perhaps the most significant event the world ever experienced—the Cross of Christ. Through masterful sermons by great pulpit masters, the reader will gain a greater understanding of the theological, devotional, and practical importance of the Cross of Christ.

You will be inspired and challenged by these great sermons from such famous preachers as: William E. Biederwolf, Arthur J. Gossip, John H. Jowett, Alexander Maclaren, G. Campbell Morgan, George H. Morrison, William E. Sangster, R. A. Torrey, and Charles H. Spurgeon.

CLASSIC SERMONS ON THE RESURRECTION OF CHRIST

Warren W. Wiersbe has carefully selected twelve sermons on the subject of the resurrection of Jesus Christ — the event which ensures the believer's future resurrection. The reader will be encouraged by messages from such great pulpit masters as J. Stuart Holden, H. A. Ironside, J. D. Jones, Henry P. Liddon, D. Martyn Lloyd-Jones, Alexander Maclaren, Walter A. Maier, G. Campbell Morgan, George H. Morrison, William E. Sangster, Charles H. Spurgeon, and George W. Truett.

These *Classic Sermons on the Resurrection of Christ* will undergird your faith and focus your attention on the Lord Jesus Christ, the "first fruits" from the dead. Preachers will gain inspiration, ideas, and insights into this important doctrine.

Available from your local Christian bookstore, or

P.O. Box 2607, Grand Rapids, MI 49501